THE WANDERINGS OF AN ELEPHANT HUNTER

THE NATIVE ATTACK

Frontispiece

THE
WANDERINGS OF AN
ELEPHANT HUNTER

BY

W. D. M. BELL

Bell, W. D. M.

Safari Press Inc.
Long Beach, California

© 2002 Safari Press

ISBN 1-57157-224-4

Library of Congress Catalog Card Number: 2001095488
10 9 8 7 6 5 4 3 2

Readers wishing to receive the Safari Press catalog, featuring many fine books on big-game hunting, wingshooting, and sporting firearms, should write to Safari Press Inc., P.O. Box 3095, Long Beach, CA 90803, USA. Tel: (714) 894-9080 or visit our Web site at www.safaripress.com.

CONTENTS

THE WANDERINGS OF AN ELEPHANT HUNTER

I

HUNTING THE BIG BULL ELEPHANT

THE most interesting and exciting form of elephant-hunting is the pursuit of the solitary bull. These fine old patriarchs stand close on twelve feet high at the shoulder and weigh from twelve thousand to fourteen thousand pounds or more, and carry tusks from eighty to one hundred and eighty pounds each. They are of great age, probably a hundred or a hundred and fifty years old. These enormous animals spend their days in the densest part of the bush and their nights in destroying native plantations.

It is curious that an animal of such a size, and requiring such huge quantities of food, should trouble to eat ground nuts—or peanuts, as they are called in this country. Of course, he does not pick them up singly, but plucks up the plant, shakes off the loose earth and eats the roots with the nuts adhering to them. One can imagine the feelings of a native when he discovers that during the night his plantation has been visited by an elephant.

The dense part of the bush where the elephant passes his day is often within half a mile of his nightly depredations, and it is only through generations of experience that these wicked old animals are enabled to carry on their marauding life. Many bear with them the price of their experience in the shape of bullets and iron spearheads ; the natives set traps for them also, the deadliest one being the falling spear. Of all devices for killing elephants known to primitive man this is the most efficient. The head and shank of the spear are made by the native blacksmith, and the whole thing probably weighs about four hundred pounds and requires eight men to haul it into position. To set the trap a spot is chosen in the forest where an elephant-path passes under a suitable tree. A sapling of some twelve feet in length is then cut. One end is made to fit tightly into the socket of the spearhead and to the other end is attached a rope. The spear end of the rope is then placed over a high bough at a point directly over the path, while the other end is taken down to one side of the path, then across it and made fast to a kind of trigger mechanism. It is placed at such a height from the ground as will allow buffalo and antelope to pass under it but not a full-grown elephant. He will have to push it out of his way. This part of the rope is generally made of a bush vine or creeper. If all goes well, an elephant comes along the path, catches the creeper on his forehead or chest, pushes it sufficiently to snap it off, and then down hurtles the huge spear, descending point first with terrific force on neck, shoulder or ribs. I have seen taken from an old bull's neck a piece of iron three feet long and almost eaten away. The wound had completely healed and it may have been there for years. If, however, the spear strikes the spine, death is instantaneous.

To get within hearing distance of these old elephants is comparatively easy. You simply pick up the enormous tracks in the early morning and follow them into their stronghold. Sometimes, after going quite a short distance through fairly open forest, you begin to find it more and more difficult to force your way along. The tracks are still there, but everything gives way before the elephant and closes in behind him again. Here in the dark cool parts there are no flies, so that the flapping and banging of ears, the usual warning of an elephant's presence, are lacking. The light begins to fail; air currents are non-existent, or so light they cannot be felt; the silence is profound. Monkeys and parrots are away in the more open parts. You may expect to hear your game at any moment now. You hope to see him, but your luck is in if you do. At the most you will see a high and ghostly stern flitting through the undergrowth, sometimes disconcertingly close in front of you. Literally nothing indicates the presence of such an enormous animal, and if it were not for the swish of the bush as it closes in behind him you would find it hard to believe that he was so close. His feet, softly cushioned with spongy gristle, make no sound. He seems to know that his stern is invulnerable alike to bullets or spears; while his huge ears, acting as sound-collecting discs, catch with their wide expanse the slightest sound of an enemy. He shows no sign of panic; there is no stampede as with younger elephants when they are disturbed; only a quiet, persistent flitting away. You may concentrate on going quietly; you may, and probably do, discard your leg gear in order to make less sound; you redouble your stealth; all in vain. He knows the game and will play hide-and-seek with you all day long and day after day. Not that this silent retreat is his only resource—by no means—he can in an instant become a roaring, headlong devil. The transformation from that silent, rakish, slinking stern to high-thrown head, gleaming tusks and whirling trunk, now advancing directly upon you, is a nerve test of the highest order. The noise is terrific. With his trunk he lashes the bushes. His great sides crash the trees down in

This spear, weighing about four hundred pounds and provided with a twelve-foot shaft, is hung head downwards from a tree. The rope, of vine or creeper, which holds it up, is stretched across an elephant-path, so that, in passing, the animal must snap it, liberating the spear to drop upon his own head or ribs.

every direction, dragging with them in their fall innumerable creepers. The whole forest is in an uproar. Much of this clatter the experienced hunter writes off as bluff, for after a short, sharp rush of this sort he will often come to a dead stop and listen intently. Here, again, his long experience has taught him that his enemy will now be in full retreat, and in most cases he is right. Certainly no native hunter waits to see, and most white men will find they have an almost uncontrollable desire to turn and flee, if only for a short way. With the deadliest of modern rifles it is only a very fleeting chance that one gets at his brain. The fact that the distance at which his head emerges from the masses of foliage is so small, and the time so short until he is right over you, in fact, makes this kind of hunting the most exciting and interesting of any in Africa, or the world, as I think most men who have experienced it will agree. If the shot at the brain is successful the monster falls and the hunter is rewarded with two magnificent tusks. And great will be the rejoicing among the natives at learning of his death, not only for the feast of meat, but also to know that their plantations have been rid of the marauding pest.

THE BRAIN SHOT AT ELEPHANT

THE hunting of the African elephant is now restricted in so many ways that it is difficult for anyone to gain experience in the shooting of them. In most of the protectorates or dependencies of the European powers a licence to kill two in a year costs from £40 to £80. It therefore behoves the sportsman to make a good job of it when he does come face to face with these splendid animals.

Twenty-five years ago parts of Africa were still open to unrestricted hunting, and it is from a stock of experience—gathered during years devoted to this fascinating pursuit—that I am about to draw, in the hope that it may assist the sportsman to bring about a successful termination to his hunt and perhaps save some unfortunate animal from a lingering death due to wounds.

In hunting elephant, as in other things, what will suit one man may not suit another. Every hunter has different methods and uses different rifles. Some believe in the big bores, holding that the bigger the bore therefore the greater the shock. Others hold that the difference between the shock from a bullet of, say, 250 grs. and that from a bullet of, say, 500 grs. is so slight that, when exercised upon an animal of such bulk as an elephant, it amounts to nothing at all. And there is no end to the arguments and contentions brought forward by either side ; therefore it should be borne in mind when reading the following instructions that they are merely the result of one individual's personal experience and not the hard and fast rules of an exact science.

As regards rifles, I will simply state that I have tried the following : ·416, ·450/·400, ·360, ·350, ·318, ·275 and ·256. At the time

I possessed the double ·400 I also had a ·275. Sometimes I used one and sometimes the other, and it began to dawn on me that when an elephant was hit in the right place with the ·275 it died just as quickly as when hit with the ·400, and, *vice versa*, when the bullet from either rifle was wrongly placed death did not ensue. In pursuance of this train of thought I wired both triggers of the double ·450/·400 together, so that when I pulled the rear one both barrels went off simultaneously. By doing this I obtained the equivalent of 800 grs. of lead propelled by 120 grs. of cordite. The net result was still the same. If wrongly placed, the 800 grs. from the ·400 had no more effect than the 200 grs. from the ·275. For years after that I continued to use the ·275 and the ·256 in all kinds of country and for all kinds of game. Each hunter should use the weapon he has *most confidence* in.

The deadliest and most humane method of killing the African elephant is the shot in the brain. Its advantages over the body shot are numerous, but among them may be mentioned that it causes instantaneous death, and no movement of the stricken animal communicates panic to others in the vicinity. The mere falling of the body from the upright to a kneeling or lying position does not appear in practice to have any other effect than to make the others mildly curious as to what has happened. On the other hand, if there are several elephants together and the heart shot is employed, the one hit almost invariably rushes off with a groan and squirm for fifty or a hundred yards, taking with him his companions, which do not stop when he stops, but continue their flight for miles. Another great advantage that the brain shot has over the heart shot is that with the former there is no search for the dead animal, whereas with the latter it is sometimes extremely difficult to find it in thick bush even when lying within fifty or sixty yards of the spot from which the shot was fired. Again, the smallest bore rifles with cartridges of a modern military description, such as the ·256, ·275, ·303 or ·318, are quite sufficiently powerful for the brain shot. The advantages of these I need hardly enumerate, such as their cheapness, reliability, handiness, lightness, freedom from recoil, etc. For the brain shot only bullets with an unbroken metal envelope (*i.e.*, solids) should be employed; and those showing good weight, moderate velocity, with a blunt or round-nosed point, are much better than the more modern high velocity sharp-pointed variety. They keep a truer course, and are not so liable to turn over as the latter.

The greatest disadvantage the brain shot has is the difficulty of locating the comparatively small brain in the enormous head. The best way is, of course, to kill an elephant by the heart shot and very carefully to dissect the head, thereby finding out the position of the brain in relation to the prominent points or marks on the head, such as the eyes and ear holes. Unfortunately for this scheme, the head is never in the same position when the animal is dead as when alive, as an elephant hardly ever dies kneeling when a body shot has been given him.

The experienced elephant shot can reach the brain from almost any angle, and with the head in almost any position. But the novice will be well advised to try the broadside shot only. Having mastered this and studied the frontal shot, he may then try it. When successful with the above two shots he may be able to reach the zenith of the elephant hunter's ambition, *i.e.*, to kill instantaneously any of these huge pachyderms with one tiny nickel pencil-like bullet when moving or stationary and from any angle.

From the point of view of danger to the hunter, should a miss occur, an ineffective shot in the head does not appear to have the enraging effect a body shot elsewhere than in the vitals sometimes has. Should the bullet miss the brain, but still pass sufficiently close to it to stun the animal, he will drop to every appearance dead. If no convulsive jerking of the limbs is noticed he is only stunned, and should be given another shot, as otherwise he will soon get up and make off as if nothing had touched him.

III

THE BODY SHOT AT ELEPHANT

ALTHOUGH the brain shot is speedier in result and more humane if bungled than the body shot, yet the latter is not to be despised. Many hunters employ no other. These will generally be found to be adherents to the " Big Bore " school. The heart and lungs of an elephant present, together with the huge arteries immediately adjacent, a large enough target for anyone, provided his or her nerves are sufficiently controlled to allow of the rifle being aimed at the correct spot. If this is not the case, and the whole animal is treated as the target, to be hit anywhere, then the result will be flight or a charge on the part of the elephant. Should the latter occur in thick stuff or high grass—12 ft. or 14 ft.— the novice will have a very unpleasant time indeed. An angry bull elephant is a magnificent sight, but an extremely difficult animal to deal with, even for the practised shot. For one thing, he is generally end on and the head is at a high angle and never still. If the novice comes through the encounter undamaged he will either leave elephants severely alone for the rest of his life or he will be extremely careful where he puts his bullet next time.

The natural inclination of most men is to fire and fire quickly, straight at the beast, anywhere. *This must be resisted* at all costs. If you can force yourself to wait until you have counted ten *slowly*, the animal is yours. The mere act of asserting your mentality gives such ascendency to your powers of judgment and such confidence that you will be surprised to find yourself coolly waiting for a better chance than the one you were quite prepared to take a few seconds before. *When* you are in this state of mind, try and get to a range of about thirty yards at right angles to the fore and aft line of the animal. Now see if the fore leg is clearly visible for the greater part. If it is and is fairly upright you may use its centre line as your *direction*. A third of the distance from the brisket to the top of the back is the *elevation*. If struck there or thereabouts either the top of the heart or the lungs or some of the arteries will be pierced and the animal cannot live, even when the bullet used is as small as a ·256. He may run fifteen or twenty yards, subside into a walk for another forty or fifty yards, stand about for some time and then subside. This is a pierced artery. He may rush away for thirty to sixty yards at a great pace and fall in his stride. This is a heart shot. Or he may rush off spouting bright red blood from his trunk in great quantities. This is a shot in the lungs.

If you have missed the deadly area and are high, you may have touched the spinal column. But it is so massive at this spot in a large elephant that it will rarely be broken, so that even when he comes down he will soon recover and be up and off. Too far forward you may get the point of the shoulder and your bullet may have so weakened the bone that when he starts off it may break. An elephant can neither trot nor gallop, but can only pace, therefore one broken leg anchors him. It is true that he may just stagger along for a few yards by substituting his tusks as a support in place of the broken leg. In a case of this sort you will naturally dispatch him as quickly as possible.

If your bullet has gone too far back and got into the stomach you may be in for a lively time, as nothing seems to anger them more than a shot so placed. If he comes for you meaning business, no instructions would help you, simply because you wouldn't have time to think of them. Hit him hard quickly and as often as you can, about a line between the eyes, or in the throat when his head is up, and see what happens. Never turn your back to him. While you can see him you know where he is. And besides, you cannot run in thick stuff without falling. Always stand still and shoot whichever animal threatens you most is what I have found to be the best plan.

Should you come upon a good bull in a position such as is shown in Fig. 1, you may kill him with a shot where the windpipe finally enters the chest as indicated by the spear. For some reason or other this is not an easy shot. It may be because the spot is nearly always in deep shadow. Personally I would wait until he lowered his head and gave me a chance at his brain. A hunting companion of mine once shot an elephant in the brain while in a position such as shown in Fig. 1. The bullet had entered through the top of the palate, showing that he must have been almost under the animal's head when he fired. In Fig. 2 we have elephant in country most suitable for the body shot, that is, open, short grassy plains. The mature bull on the right is the first choice. Observe his massive head, short but heavy tusks. He is not old, but his teeth will weigh well. The second choice is the one on the left which is swinging his ears. Our friend in the middle which is philandering with the heavy-looking cow should be spared. Observe how his teeth taper away to nothing. They would scarcely scale 30 lb. each.

In Fig. 3 I have tried to show what happens when you aim your rifle *with one eye closed* at an elephant's brain. Everything below the head is obliterated with this form of backsight. This makes it much more difficult to judge correctly the position of the brain, as the sight cuts out one or both of the " leading marks," *i.e.*, the eye and the earhole. The shaded portion represents the hands holding the rifle.

Fig. 4 is meant to show what happens when the same sight is being taken at the same elephant but *with both eyes open*. Owing to the left eye seeing the whole image—as its view of it is not obstructed by the hands—the whole of the elephant's head appears visible *through the hands and rifle*. The advantage is obvious. Anyone can do it who will take the trouble to practise.

Finally, I would like to warn anyone who may be going out for his elephant for the first time to beware that the native gun-bearer does not rush him into *firing too soon*. They have not our medical knowledge which teaches us that the brain, heart and lungs are the best places to hit. They would hit them anywhere and trust to "medicine" to do the rest. I have been solemnly assured by native elephant hunters that it is not the bullet which causes the animal's death, but the fire from the powder which enters the hole made by the bullet.

IV

AFRICAN "MEDICINE" OR WITCHCRAFT AND ITS BEARING ON SPORT

THE ruling factor in the pagan African's life is witchcraft, generally called throughout the continent "medicine." All his doings are ruled by it. No venture can be undertaken without it. Should he be going into the bush on some trivial project he will pick up a stone and deposit it on what has through years become a huge pile. This is to propitiate some spirit. But this apparently does not fully ensure the success of the expedition, for should a certain species of bird call on the wrong side of the road the whole affair is off and he returns to his village to wait until another day when the omens are good.

In illness he recognises no natural laws; all is ascribed to medicine on the part of some enemy. Should his wife fail to produce the yearly baby, someone is making medicine against him through her. Hunting or raiding ventures are never launched without weeks of medicine making. The regular practitioners of this medicine are called "medicine men" or witch doctors. Their power is enormous and is hardly fully realised even by the European administrations, although several African penal codes now contain legislative efforts to curtail the practice of the evil eye and the black arts. These medicine men have always appeared to me to be extremely shrewd and cunning men who yet really believed in their powers. While all goes well their lot is an enviable one. Gifts of food are showered upon them. I suspect that they secretly eat the fowls and goats which are brought as sacrifices to propitiate the spirits : at any rate, these seem to disappear in a mysterious manner. Beer and women are theirs for the asking as long as all goes well.

But, should the medicine man have a run of ill luck in his practice and be not too firmly established, he sometimes comes to grief. The most frequent cause of their downfall appears to occur in the foretelling of rain.   Supposing a dry year happens to come along, as it so frequently does in Africa, everyone to save his crops resorts to the medicine man.   They take to him paltry presents to begin with.   No rain.   They give him fowls, sheep and goats.   Still no rain.   They discuss it among themselves and conclude that he is not yet satisfied.   More presents are given to him and, maybe, he is asked why he has not yet made the rain come.   Never at a loss, he explains that there is a strong combination up against him, a very strong one, with which he is battling day and night.   If he only had a bullock to sacrifice to such and such a spirit he might be able to overcome the opposition.   And so it goes on.   Cases are known among rich tribes where the medicine man has enriched himself with dozens of head of cattle and women.   At this stage should rain appear all is well, and the medicine man is acclaimed the best of fellows and the greatest of the fraternity.   But should its appearance be so tardy that the crops fail, then that medicine man has lost his job and has to flee to some far tribe.   If he be caught he will, most probably, be stoned or clubbed to death.

To the elephant hunter the medicine man can sometimes be of great assistance.   I once consulted a medicine man about a plague of honey-guides.   These are African birds about the size of a yellowhammer, which have the extraordinary habit of locating wild bees' nests and leading man to them by fluttering along in front of him, at the same time keeping up a continuous and penetrating twittering until the particular tree in which the nest is situated is reached.   After the native has robbed the nest of its honey, by the aid of smoke and fire, he throws on the ground a portion—sometimes very small—of the grub-filled comb as a reward for the bird.

My experience occurred just after the big bush fires, when elephant are so easily tracked, their spoor standing out grey on the blackened earth.   At this season, too, the bees' nests contain honey and grubs. Hundreds of natives roam the bush and the honey-guides are at their busiest. Elephants were numerous, and for sixteen days I tracked them down and either saw or heard them stampede, warned of our presence by honey-guides, without the chance of a shot. Towards the end of this ghastly period my trackers were completely discouraged. They urged me to consult the medicine man, and I agreed to do so, thinking that at any rate my doing so would imbue the boys with fresh hope. Arrived at the village, in due course I visited the great man. His first remark was that he knew that I was coming to consult him, and that he also knew the reason of my visit. By this he thought to impress me, I suppose, but, of course, he had heard all about the honey-guides from my boys, although they stoutly denied it when I asked them after the interview was over. Yes, I said, I had come to see him about those infernal birds. And I told him he could have all the meat of the first elephant I killed if he could bring about that desirable end to my long hunt. He said he would fix it up. And so he did, and the very next day, too.

In the evening of the day upon which I had my consultation I was strolling about the village while my boys got food, prepared for another trip in the bush. Besides these preparations I noticed a lot of basket mending and sharpening of knives. One woman I questioned said she was coming with us on the morrow to get some elephant meat. I spoke to two or three others. They were all preparing to smoke and dry large quantities of meat, and they were all going with us. Great optimism prevailed everywhere. Even I began to feel that the turning in the lane was in sight. Late that night one of my trackers came to say that the medicine man wished me to stay in camp in the morning and not to proceed as I had intended. I asked the reason of this and he simply said that the medicine man was finding elephant for me and that when the sun was about so high (9 o'clock) I should hear some news.

Soon after daybreak natives from the village began to arrive in camp. All seemed in great spirit, and everyone came with knives, hatchets, baskets and skin bags of food.   They sat about in groups laughing and joking among themselves.   Breakfast finished, the boys got everything ready for the march.   What beat me was that everyone—my people included—seemed certain they were going somewhere.   About 9.30 a native glistening with sweat arrived. He had seen elephant.   How many?   Three!   Big ones?   Yes! Hurriedly telling the chief to keep his people well in the rear, off we set at a terrific pace straight through the bush until our guide stopped by a tree.   There he had left his companion watching the elephants.   Two or three hundred yards further on we came to their tracks.   Everywhere were the welcome signs of their having fed as they went.   But, strangest thing of all, not a single honey-guide appeared.   Off again as hard as we could go, the tracks running on ahead clear and distinct, light grey patches on a burnt ground with the little grey footmarks of the native ahead of us.   In an hour or so we spotted him in a tree, and as we drew near we caught the grey glint of elephant.   Still no honey-guides; blessings on the medicine man!   Wind right, bush fairly open, it only remained to see if they were warrantable.   That they were large bulls we already knew from their tracks.   Leaving the boys, I was soon close behind the big sterns as they wandered gently along. In a few seconds I had seen their ivory sufficiently to know that one was really good and the other two quite shootable beasts. Now for the brain shot.   Of all thrills in the world give me the standing within 20 yds. of good elephant, waiting for a head to turn to send a tiny nickel bullet straight to the brain.   From toe-nail to top of back they were all a good 11 ft.   Stepping a few yards to the left and keeping parallel with them I saw that the way to bag the lot was to shoot the leader first, although he was not the biggest.   Letting pass one or two chances at the middle and rear-most beasts, I finally got a bullet straight into the leader's brain. The middle one turned towards the shot and the nearest turned away from it, so that they both presented chances at their brains : the former an easy broadside standing, the latter a behind the ear shot and running. So hard did this one come down on his tusks that one of them was loose in its socket and could be drawn straight out. Almost immediately one could hear a kind of rush coming through the bush. The chief and his people were arriving. There seemed to be hundreds of them. And the noise and rejoicings! I put guards on the medicine man's beast. From first to last no honey-guide had appeared. The reader must judge for himself whether there was any magic in the affair or not. What I think happened was this: knowing that the medicine man was taking the affair in hand and that he had promised elephant, the natives believed that elephant would be killed. Believing that, they were willing to look industriously for them in the bush. Great numbers of them scattered through the bush had the effect of splitting up and scattering the honey-guides, besides increasing the chances of finding elephant. The fact that we did not hear a single bird must have been mere chance, I think. But you could not convince an African of that. Natural causes and their effects have not a place in his mind. I remember once an elephant I had hit in the heart shook his head violently in his death throes. I was astounded to see one of his tusks fly out and land twelve paces away. The boys were awe-stricken when they saw what had happened. After ten minutes' silence they started whispering to each other and then my gun-bearer came to speak to me. He solemnly warned me with emotion in his voice never to go near another elephant. If I did it would certainly kill me after what had occurred. It was quite useless my pointing out that the discarded tusk was badly diseased, and that it would have probably fallen out in a short time anyhow. No! No! Bwana, it is medicine! said they.

Some few years ago I was hunting in the Wa Boni country in British East Africa. The Wa Boni form an offshoot of the Sanya tribe and are purely hunters, having no fixed abode and never undertaking cultivation of any kind. They will not even own stock of any sort, holding that such ownership leads to trouble in the form of—in the old days—raids, and now taxation. Living entirely on the products of the chase, honey, bush fruits and vegetables, they are perhaps the most independent people in the world. They are under no necessity to combine for purposes of defence, having nothing to defend. Owning no plantations, they are independent of droughts. The limitless bush provides everything they want. Skins for wearing apparel, meat for eating, fibres of great strength for making string and ropes for snares, sinew for bowstrings, strong and tough wood for bows, clay for pottery, grass for shelter, water-tubers for drinking when water is scarce, fruit foods of all sorts; and all these for the gathering. No wonder they are reluctant to give up their roving life. I was living in one of the M'Boni villages, if village it could be called. It consisted of, perhaps, twenty grass shelters dotted here and there under the trees. It was the season when honey is plentiful, and there was a great deal of drinking of honey mead going on. This is simply made by mixing honey with water and supplying a ferment to it. There are several ferments in the bush, but on this particular occasion the seeds of the wild tree-calabash were being used. On the third day after brewing the mead is very intoxicating. A native will drink great quantities before getting really drunk, but when he does reach that stage he appears to remain so for many hours. I was once among a very wild and treacherous tribe where drunkenness was very prevalent. A nude gentleman about 6 ft. 5 ins. in height strolled into camp one day accompanied by his daughter. In his hand he carried two beautifully polished thrusting spears. The bartering of variously coloured beads, brass and iron wire, etc., for native flour was going on in camp. Watching this, our friend suddenly stooped down, snatched a handful of beads and made off with them in a leisurely manner. Immediately there was an uproar from my people, and a dozen boys gave chase to try to recover the stolen goods. At the same time the affair was reported to me in my tent. On emerging, I saw the tall black savage stalking across the open ground with a howling mob of my porters round him. Without turning to the right or left and without hurry he kept his two

10 ft. spears darting in all directions, and none could close with him.   Something had to be done.   At first I thought of doing something silly with a rifle, and then I had a brain-wave.   I shouted to the boys to stone him.   They jumped to the idea, and in three seconds that scoffing barbarian had his tail down and was running for dear life, amid all roars of laughter from both sides.   Unluckily for him a rock weighing several pounds caught him on the back of the neck and over he went.   Like a pack of terriers, my lads were on him, and presently he was borne back in triumph to camp.   His strength was so prodigious and his naked body so covered in sheep's fat that it took a dozen men to hold him.   A public thrashing was

M'SANYA BOW AND POISONED ARROW.

The poisoned part is carried, separately, from the shank, carefully wrapped in buckskin.

now administered, in order to show the tribe that that kind of game would not do.   But being quite drunk the only effect of the thrashing was to make the victim sing and laugh.   This rather spoilt the effect of the whole thing, so I gave orders to tie him up until he was sober.   Thus he passed the night, singing the whole time.   Nothing could be done to silence him, but the camp guards kept pouring buckets of cold water over him to try to sober him up.   In spite of this he was still supremely drunk next morning when we let him go.

One morning early, news came in to the Boni village that the tracks of two large bull elephants were to be seen not far off. Arrived at the tracks, it was evident that they had passed along there during the night.   Soon the welcome signs of their having fed as they went were seen.   Promising as these signs were, it was not until midday that we began to come up with them.   Presently the tracks led us into a patch of dense evergreen forest, and here we expected to find them.   Leaving my companions near the edge of the forest, I went in on the tracks as silently yet as quickly as possible. I went quickly because the wind was tricky, and it is always better on these occasions to get to close quarters as soon as you can, thereby lessening the chances of your game winding you.   I was soon within hearing distance of the elephants.   As I lifted my leg cautiously over some tangle of bush I could hear a deep sigh or an internal rumble from the dozing animals.   Turning a bush the following scene disclosed itself.   A small native boy was in the act of pinking an enormous elephant with his tiny reed arrow.   Aiming for the big intestine of the father beast he let drive before I could stop him.   In an instant all was uproar.   The two elephants stampeded madly through the forest, crashing everything down in front of them, disappearing in a cloud of pollen, dust and leaves.   The formerly still and sleepy bush seemed alive with crying monkeys and calling birds as the little boy proceeded coolly to pick up his guinea-fowl arrow where it had fallen after failing to pierce the elephant's hide.

"Hullo, you little devil," I said.

A half glance round and he was gone.   The little sportsman had been simply amusing himself.   Of course, the grown men of the Wa Boni kill elephants, but for this they use extraordinarily heavy arrows which require immensely powerful bows to propel them.   Some of these bows require a pull of 100 lb. to get them out to the end of the wooden arrow where the poisoned part fits into a socket.   There is some peculiar knack in this, as no other native I have seen—and certainly no white man—can get them more than half way, and yet these natives are very small and slight.

V

KARAMOJO

I.—INTO THE UNKNOWN

MY earliest recollection of myself is that of a child whose sole ambition in life was to hunt. At a very early age I conceived the idea of hunting the American bison. With this end in view I gathered together a few oddments, such as the barrels of a double-barrelled pistol, a clasp knife, a few bits of string and all the money—chiefly pennies—that I could lay hands on. This bison-hunting expedition was prematurely cut short at the Port of Glasgow by the critical state of its finances, for after buying a pork pie for twopence its treasury was found to be almost empty. This was a sad blow, and it was while thinking it over on a doorstep that a kindly policeman instituted proceedings which resulted in the lost and crestfallen child being restored to his family. But the growth of years and the acquirement of the art of reading— by which I discovered that bison no longer existed in America—my ambition became fixed on becoming an elephant hunter. The reading of Gordon Cumming's books on Africa finished the business. An elephant hunter I determined to become; this idea never left me. Finally, after all kinds of vicissitudes I arrived in Africa and heard of a wonderful new and unexplored country called Karamojo. Elephants were reported by the black traders to be very numerous with enormous tusks, and there was no sort of administration to hamper the hunter with restrictions and game laws. Above all there appeared to be no other person hunting elephants in this Eldorado except the natives, and they had no firearms. My informants told me that the starting point for all

20

safaris (caravans) was Mumias, a native town and Government Post at the foot of Mount Elgon, which formed the last outpost of civilisation for a traveller proceeding North.

At the time of which I write Mumias was a town of some importance. It was the base for all trading expeditions to the Lake Rudolph basin, Turkana, Dabossa and the Southern Abyssinia country. In the first few years of the trade in ivory this commodity was obtained for the most trifling sums; for instance, a tusk worth £50 or £60 could be bought for two or three shillings' worth of beads or iron wire. As time went on and more traders flocked to Karamojo to share. in the huge profits of the ivory trade, competition became keener. Prices rose higher and higher. Where once beads and iron wire sufficed to buy a tusk, now a cow must be paid. Traders were obliged to go further and further afield to find new territory until they came in violent contact with raiding parties of Abyssinians away in the far North.

When most of the dead ivory in the country had been traded off the only remaining source was the yearly crop of tusks from the elephants snared and killed by the native Karamojans. For these comparatively few tusks competition became so keen and prices so high that there was no longer any profit when as much as eight or ten cows had to be paid for a large tusk, and the cows bought down at the base for spot cash and at prices of from £2 to £5 each. Hence arose the idea in the brains of two or three of the bolder spirits among the traders to take by force that which they could no longer afford to buy. Instead of traders they became raiders. In order to ensure success to a raid an alliance would be made with some tribe which was already about equal in strength to its neighbours through centuries of intertribal warfare. The addition of three or four hundred guns to the tribe's five or six thousand spearmen rendered the result of this raid by the combined forces almost beyond doubt, and moreover, conferred upon the raiders such complete domination of the situation that they were able to search out and capture the young girls, the acquisition of which is the great aim and object of all activity in the Moham-medan mind.

Complete and magnificent success attending the first raiding venture the whole country changed magically. The hitherto more or less peaceful looking trading camps gave place to huge armed Bomas surrounded by high thorn fences. Everyone—trader or native—went about armed to the teeth. Footsore or sick travellers from caravans disappeared entirely, or their remains were found by the roadside. Native women and cattle were heavily guarded, for no man trusted a stranger.

Into this country of suspicion and brooding violence I was about to venture. As soon as my intention became known among the traders at Mumias I encountered on every side a firm barrage of lies and dissuasion of every sort. The buying of pack donkeys was made impossible. Guides were unobtainable. Information about the country north of Turkwell was either distorted and false or entirely withheld. I found that no Mohammedan boy would engage with me. The reason for all this apparently malicious obstruction on the part of the trading community was not at the time known to me, but it soon became clear when I had crossed the Turkwell and found that the peaceful, polite and prosperous looking trader of Mumias became the merciless and bloody Dacoit as soon as he had crossed that river and was no longer under Euro-pean control. Numbering among them, as they did, some pretty notorious ex-slavers, they knew how unexpectedly far the arm of the law could sometimes reach and they no doubt foresaw that nothing but trouble would arise from my visit to the territory they had come to look upon as theirs by right of discovery. It surprises me now, when I think of how much they had at stake, that they resorted to no more stringent methods than those related above to prevent my entry into Karamojo. As it was I soon got together some bullocks and some pagan boys. The bullocks I half trained to carry packs and the Government Agent very kindly arranged that I should have eight Snider rifles with which to defend myself, and to instil confidence among my Baganda and Wanyamwere and Kavirondo boys. The Sniders looked well and no one knew except myself that the ammunition for them was all bad. And then I had my personal rifles, at that time a ·303 Lee-Enfield, a ·275 Rigby-Mauser and a double ·450-·400, besides a Mauser pistol which could be used as a carbine and which soon acquired the name of " Bom-Bom " and a reputation for itself equal to a hundred ordinary rifles.

While searching through some boxes of loose ammunition in the store at Mumias in the hope of finding at least a few good rounds for my Snider carbines I picked up a Martini-Henry cartridge, and while looking at its base it suddenly struck me that possibly it could be fired from a Snider. And so it proved to be. The base being ·577 calibre fitted perfectly, but the bullet, being only ·450 bore, was scarcely what you might call a good fit for a ·577 barrel, and there was, of course, no accuracy to the thing at all. But it went off with a bang and the propensity of its bullet to fly off at the most disconcerting angles after rattling through the barrel from side to side seemed just to suit the style of aiming adopted by my eight askaris (soldiers), for on several occasions jackal and hyena were laid low while prowling round the camp at night.

Bright and early next morning my little safari began to get itself ready for the voyage into the Unknown. The loads were got out and lined up. First of all an askari, with a Snider rifle very proud in a hide belt with five Martini cartridges gleaming yellow in it. He had carefully polished them with sand for the occasion. Likewise the barrel of the old Snider showed signs of much rubbing, and a piece of fat from the tail of a sheep dangled by a short string from the hammer. Then my chop-boxes, and camp gear borne by porters, followed by my boy Suede and Sulie-man, the cook, of cannibal parentage be it whispered. As usual, all the small loads seemed to be jauntily and lightly perched on the massive heads and necks of the biggest porters, while the big loads looked doubly big in comparison to the spindly shanks which appeared below them. One enormous porter in particular drew my attention. He was capering about in the most fantastic manner with a large box on his head. From the rattle which proceeded from the box I perceived that this was the cook's mate, and as I possessed only a few aluminium cooking pots, his was perhaps the lightest load of any, and I vowed that he should have a good heavy tusk to carry as soon as possible. This I was enabled to do soon after passing the Turkwell, and this splendid head-carrier took entire charge of a tusk weighing 123 lb., carrying it with pride for several hundred weary miles on a daily ration of 1 lb. of mtama grain and unlimited buck meat.

Usually when a safari started from Mumias for the "Barra" —as the bush or wilderness is called—the townsfolk would turn out with drums and horns to give them a send off, but in our case we departed without any demonstration of that sort. We passed through almost deserted and silent streets, and we struck out for the Turkwell, the trail skirting the base of Elgon for six days, as we travelled slowly, being heavily laden. I was able to find and shoot enough haartebeeste and oribi to keep the safari in meat, and after two or three days' march the boys became better and better and the bullocks more and more docile. I purposely made the marches more easy at first in order to avoid sore backs, and it was easy to do so, as there were good streams of water crossing our path every few miles.

On the seventh day we reached the Turkwell River. After descending several hundred feet from the high plateau we crossed by the ford and pitched camp on the opposite or north bank. The Turkwell has its sources in the crater of Elgon and its slopes. Its waters reach the dry, hot plains of Karamojo after a drop of about 9,000 ft. in perhaps twenty or thirty miles. In the dry season— when it is fordable almost anywhere—it totally disappears into its sandy river bed while still some days' march from its goal, Lake Rudolph. It is a queer and romantic river, for it starts in lava 14,000 ft. above sea-level, traverses bitterly cold and often snow-covered heath land, plunges down through the dense bamboo belt, then through dark and dripping evergreen forest to emerge on the sandy plains of Karamojo. From this point to Rudolph its banks are clothed with a more or less dense belt of immense flat-topped thorn trees interspersed with thickets of every kind of thorny bush, the haunt of rhino, buffalo and elephant. Throughout its entire course its waters were drunk, at the time of which I write, by immense herds of elephant during the dry season. Even after disappearing underground, elephant and natives easily procured water by simply making holes in the soft clean sands of its river bed.

At that time the Turkwell formed the northern boundary of European rule. North of it was no rule but disrule. The nearest cultivated settlement of Karamojo natives was at Mani-Mani, some 150 miles to the north, but scattered about in the bush were many temporary settlements of poor Karamojans who got their living by hunting and snaring everything from elephant downwards.

Dreadful tales of murders of peaceful travellers had been related by Swahilis, and we were careful not to let anyone straggle far from the main body. At night my eight askaris mounted guard and kept a huge fire going. Their vigilance was extraordinary, and their keenness and cheerfulness, fidelity and courage of a very high order, showing them to be born soldiers. Their shooting was simply atrocious, in spite of practice with a ·22 I had, but notwithstanding their inability to align and aim a rifle properly, they used sometimes to bring off the most brilliant shots under the most impossible conditions of shooting light, thereby showing a great natural aptitude to point a gun and time the shot.

While we were drying out the gear that had got wet while crossing the Turkwell two natives strolled into the camp. These were the first Karamojans we had seen, and I was very much interested in them. They showed great independence of bearing as they stood about leaning on their long thrusting spears. I had some difficulty in getting into conversation with them, although I had an excellent interpreter.   They seemed very taciturn and suspicious.   However, I got it explained to them that I had come for one purpose only, *i.e.*, to hunt elephant.   They admitted that there were plenty of elephant, but when I asked them to show me where to look for them they merely asked me how I proposed to kill them when I did see them.   On showing them my rifle they laughed, and said they had seen Swahili traders using those things for elephants and, although they killed men well enough, they were useless against elephant.   My answer to this was that I had procured some wonderful medicine which enabled me to kill the largest-sized elephant with one shot, and that if they would like to see this medicine working all they had to do was to show me where the elephant were and that I would do the rest and they should have as much meat as they wanted.   They retorted that if my medicine was truly sufficiently powerful to kill an elephant instantaneously, then they could not believe that it would fail to show me their whereabouts also.   This grave fault in my medicine had to be explained, and I could only say that I grieved heartily over the deficiency, which I attributed to the jealousy of a medicine man who was a rival of him who had given me the killing medicine. This left them not altogether satisfied, but a better impression was produced when I presented them with a quarter of buck meat, while telling them that I killed that kind of meat every day.   They went off without holding out any hope of showing me elephant, and I thought that I had seen the last of them.   I sat until late in my long chair by the camp fire under a brilliant sky and wonderful moon listening to the talk of my Nzamwezi boys and wondering how we were going to fare in the real wild land ahead of us.

An early start was made next morning and we had covered perhaps six or seven miles when the two natives, visitors to our camp of yesterday, came stalking along appearing to cover the ground at a great rate without showing any hurry or fuss.   I stopped and called the interpreter and soon learned that four large elephants had that morning passed close to their camp in the bush and that when they left to call me the elephants could still be heard in the vicinity. At once I was for going, but the interpreter and the headman both cautioned me against treachery, declaring that it was only a blind to separate us preparatory to a general massacre. This view I thought a bit far fetched, but I ordered the safari to get under weigh and to travel well together until they reached the first water, where they were immediately to cut sufficient thorn trees to completely encircle themselves in camp, to keep a good look-out and to await my coming.

Taking my small boy and the gigantic cook's mate—whose feather-weight load I had transferred to the cook's head—I hastily put together a few necessities and hurried off with the two Kara-mojans at a great pace. We soon struck off from the main trail and headed for the Turkwell Valley. Straight through the open thorn bush we went, the elephant hide sandals of my native guides crunching innumerable darning-needle-sized thorns underfoot, the following porters with their light loads at a jog trot, myself at a fast but laboured walk, while the guides simply soaked along with consummate ease.

Supremely undemonstrative as natives usually are, there was yet observable a kind of suppressed excitement about their bearing, and I noticed that whenever a certain bird called on the right hand the leader would make a low remark to his companions with an indescribably satisfied kind of gesture, whereas the same calling on the left hand drew no notice from them beyond a certain increased forward resolution and a stiff ignoring of it.

The significance of these signs were lost on me at that time, but I was to come to learn them well in my later dealings with these tribes. They were omens and indicated success or failure to our hunting.

On the whole they were apparently favourable. At any rate, the pace never slackened, and I was beginning to wish for a slow-ing down. As we drew nearer the Turkwell Valley signs of elephant became more and more numerous. Huge paths worn perfectly smooth and with their edges cut as clear as those of garden walks by the huge pads of the ponderous animals began to run together, forming more deeply worn ones converging towards the drinking places on the river. Occasionally the beautiful lesser koodoo stood watching us or loped away, flirting its white fluffed tail. Once we passed a rhino standing motionless with snout ever directed towards us. A small detour round him as we did not wish to get mixed up with his sort and on again. Halt! The little line bunches up against the motionless natives. A distant rumble resembling somewhat a cart crossing a wooden bridge, and after a few seconds of silence the crash of a broken tree.

Elephant! *Atome!* (in Karamojo). Word the first to be learned and the last to be forgotten of any native language. A kind of excitement seizes us all; me most of all, the Karamojans least. Now the boys are told to stay behind and to make no noise. They are at liberty to climb trees if they like. I look to my ·303, but, of course, it had been ready for hours. Noting that the wind —what there was of it—was favourable, the natives and I go forward, and soon we come upon the broken trees, mimosa and white thorn, the chewed fibrous balls of sansivera, the moist patches with froth still on them, the still steaming and unoxidised spoor, and the huge tracks with the heavily imprinted clear-cut corrugations of a very recently passing bunch of bull elephants. In numbers they were five as nearly as I could estimate. Tracking them was child's play, and I expected to see them at any moment. It was, however, much longer than I anticipated before we sighted their dull grey hides. For they were travelling as well as feeding. It is remarkable how much territory elephant cover when thus feeding along. At first sight they seem to be so leisurely, and it is not until one begins to keep in touch with them that their speed is realised. Although they appear to take so few steps, each step of their lowest gait is about 6 ft. Then, again, in this feeding along there is *always* at least one of the party moving forward at about $3\frac{1}{2}$ miles per hour, although the other members may be stopping and feeding, then catching up again by extending the stride to 7 ft. or more.

As soon as they were in sight I got in front of the Karamojans and ran in to about 20 yds. from the stern of the rearmost animal. Intense excitement now had me with its usual signs, hard breathing through the mouth, dry palate and an intense longing to shoot.

As I arrived at this close proximity I vividly remember glancing along the grey bulging sides of the three rearmost animals, who all happened to be in motion at the same time in single file, and remarking a tusk of an incredible length and size sweeping out from the grey wall. I instantly determined to try for this one first. With extraordinary precautions against making a noise, and stoopings and contortions of the body, all of which after-experience taught me were totally unnecessary, I got away off at right-angles to the file of elephants and could now grasp the fact that they were all very large and carried superb ivory.

I was now almost light-headed with excitement, and several times on the very verge of firing a stupid and hasty shot from my jumping and flickering rifle. So shaky was it when I once or twice put it to my shoulder that even in my then state of mind I saw that no good could come of it. After a minute or two, during which I was returning to a more normal state, the animal with the largest tusks left the line slightly, and slowly settled into a halt beside a mimosa bush. I got a clear glimpse at his broadside at what looked about 20 yds., but was really 40 yds., and I fired for his heart. With a flinch, a squirm and a roar he was soon in rapid motion straight away, with his companions in full flight ahead of him. I was rather surprised at this headlong flight after one shot as I had expected the elephant here to be more unsophisticated, but hastily concluding that the Swahili traders must have been pumping lead into them more often than one imagined, I legged it for the cloud of dust where the fleeting animals had disappeared. Being clad in running shorts and light shoes, it was not long before I almost ran slap up against a huge and motionless grey stern. Recoiling very rapidly indeed from this awe-inspiring sight, I saw on one side of it an enormous head and tusk which appeared to stick out at right-angles. So drooping were the trunk and ears and so motionless the whole appearance of what had been a few seconds ago the very essence of power and activity that it was borne straight to even my inexperienced mind that here was death. And so it was, for as I stared goggle-eyed the mighty body began to sway from side to side more and more, until with a crash it fell sideways, bearing earthwards with it a fair sized tree. Straight past it I saw another elephant, turned almost broadside, at about 100 yds. distance, evidently listening and obviously on the point of flight. Running a little forward so as to get a clear sight of the second beast, I sat quickly down and fired carefully at the shoulder, when much the same performance took place as in the first case, except that No. 2 came down to a slow walk after a burst of speed instead of to a standstill as with No. 1.

Ranging rapidly alongside I quickly put him out of misery and tore after the others which were, of course, by this time, thoroughly alarmed and in full flight. After a mile or two of fast going I found myself pretty well done, so I sat down and rolled myself a cigarette of the strong black shag so commonly smoked by the Swahilis. Presently my native guides came with every appearance of satisfaction on their now beaming faces.

After a few minutes' rest we retracked the elephant back to where our two lay dead. The tusks of the first one we examined were not long but very thick, and the other had on one side a tusk broken some 2 ft. outside the lip, while on the other was the magnificent tusk which had filled me with wonder earlier on. It was almost faultless and beautifully curved. What a shame that its companion was broken!

As we were cutting the tail off, which is always done to show anyone finding the carcase that it has been killed and claimed, my good fellows came up with the gear and the interpreter. Everyone, including myself, was in high good humour, and when the

Karamojans said that their village was not far off we were more pleased than ever, especially as the sun was sinking rapidly. After what appeared to the natives no doubt as a short distance, but what seemed to my sore feet and tired legs a very long one, we saw the welcome fires of a camp and were soon sitting by one while a group of naked savages stood looking silently at the white man and his preparations for eating and sleeping. These were simple enough. A kettle was soon on the fire for tea, while some strips of sun-cured haartebeeste biltong writhed and sizzled on the embers. Meanwhile my boys got the bed ready by first of all cutting the grass and smoothing down the knobs of the ground while another spread grass on it to form a mattress. Over this the canvas sheet and blankets and with a bag of cartridges wrapped in a coat for a pillow the bed was complete. Then two forked sticks stuck in the ground close alongside the bed to hold the rifle and all was ready for the night.

II.—IVORY AND THE RAIDERS

After a hearty supper of toasted biltong and native flour porridge, washed down with tea, I cleaned my rifle, loaded it and lay down utterly tired out and soon dropped off to the music of hyenas' howling. As soon as ever it was light enough to see, we left for the dead elephant, and the way did not seem half so long in the fresh morning air as it had appeared the evening before. We quickly arrived, followed by all the villagers, men, women and children, every one in high spirits at the sight of the mountains of meat. In this country the meat of elephants is esteemed more highly than that of any other animal, as it contains much more fat. The Karamojan elephants are distinguished for their bodily size, the quality and size of their ivory and for the quantity of fat on them.

I was anxious to get the tusks out as rapidly as possible in order to rejoin my caravan, so I divided the Karamojans into two gangs and explained to them that no one was to touch the carcases until the tusks were out, but that then they could have all the meat. They set to with a will to get all the skin and flesh off the head. It is necessary to do this so as to expose the huge bone sockets containing the ends of the tusks. About a third of their length is so embedded, and a very long, tedious and hard job it is to get all the skin and gristle cut away. Nothing blunts a knife more quickly than elephant hide, because of the sand and grit in its loose texture.

When the skull is clean on one side the neck should be cut. This alone is a herculean task. The vertebra severed, the head is turned over by eight or ten men, and the other side similarly cleaned. When both sockets are ready an axe is used to chop them away chip by chip until the tusk is free. This chopping should always be done by an expert, as otherwise large chips off the tusk itself are liable to be taken by the axe.

This chopping out of ivory is seldom resorted to by natives, requiring as it does so much hard work. They prefer to leave the sun and putrefaction to do the work for them. On the third day after the death the upper tusk can usually be drawn without difficulty from the socket and the underneath one on the following day.

On this particular occasion no one was at all adept at chopping out, and it was hours before the tusks were freed. Later on my Wanzamwezi boys became very expert indeed at this job, and twelve of them, whose particular job it became, could handle as many as ten bull elephants in a day provided they were not too distant one from the other and that they had plenty of native assistance.

While the chopping out was going on I had leisure to watch the natives, and what struck me first was the remarkable difference between the men and the women. The former were tall, some of them quite 6 ft. 4 ins., slim and well made, while the latter were distinctly short, broad, beefy and squat. The married ones wore aprons of dressed buckskin tied round the waist by the legs of the skin and ornamented with coloured beads sewn on with sinew thread. The unmarried girls wore no skins at all and had merely a short fringe of black thread attached to a string round the waist and falling down in front. As regards hair, all the women wore it plaited and falling down all round the head and giving somewhat the appearance of "bobbed" hair. Some of the men wore the most extraordinary-looking periwigs made up of their own and also their ancestors' hair mixed with clay so as to form a kind of covering for the top of the head and falling down the back of the neck. In this pad of human felt were set neat little woven sockets in such a way as to hold upright an ostrich feather in each.

The people with whom we are dealing at the moment were poor and therefore hunters. Africans differ from us entirely on the question of hunting; whereas among us it is the well-off who hunt, among them it is the poor. Having nothing but a few goats and sheep, these hunters inhabit the bush, shifting their village from site to site according to the movements of the game.

Their system of taking game is the snare; their only weapon a spear. The art of snaring has been brought to a unique development by these people, for they have snares varying in size for all animals from elephant down to dik-dik.

The snare for elephant is a great hawser, $4\frac{1}{2}$ ins. in diameter, of twisted antelope or giraffe hides. One may find in the same rope haartebeeste hide, eland, zebra, rhinoceros, buffalo and giraffe hide. If made of haartebeeste alone no less than eleven or twelve skins are required. The skins are scraped and pounded with huge wooden mallets for weeks by the women before being twisted or "laid" into the rope which is to form the snare. The running nooses at both ends are beautifully made. Besides the snare there is a thing like a cart wheel without any hub and with scores of thin spokes meeting in the centre where their points are sharp. The snare is laid in the following manner :

A well frequented elephant path is chosen and somewhere near the spot decided upon for the snare a large tree is cut. Judgment in the choosing of this must be exercised as if it is too heavy the snare will break, and if too light the snared elephant will travel too far. A tree trunk which ten or twelve men can just stagger along with seems to be the thing. This log is then brought to the scene of action and at its smaller end a deep groove is cut all round to take the noose at one end of the rope. After this noose has been fitted and pulled and hammered tight—no easy matter—the log is laid at right angles to the path with the smaller end pointing towards it. A hole a good bit larger than an elephant's foot is then dug in the path itself to a depth of two feet or so. Over this hole is fitted the cart wheel. Round the rim the large noose of the snare is laid and the whole covered carefully over with earth to resemble the path again. The snare is now laid, and if all goes well some solitary old bull comes wandering along at night, places his foot on the earth borne by the sharp spokes of the hubless wheel, goes through as the spokes open downwards, lifts his foot and with it the wheel bearing the noose well up the ankle, strides forward and tightens the noose. The more he pulls the tighter draws the noose until the log at the other end of the snare begins to move. Now alarmed and presently angry, he soon gets rid of the cart wheel, but as its work is already done, that does not matter. The dragging log is now securely attached to the elephant's leg, and it is seldom that he gets rid of it unless it should jamb in rocks or trees. Soon he becomes thoroughly alarmed and sets off at a great pace, the log ploughing along behind him. Should a strong, vigorous young bull become attached to a rather light log, he may go twenty or thirty miles.

As soon as it becomes known to the natives that an elephant has been caught, everyone within miles immediately seizes all his spears and rushes to the spot where the snare had been set and from there eagerly takes up the trail of the log. When they come up with the somewhat exhausted animal they spear it to death. Then every scrap of meat is shared among the village which owns the snare, the tusks becoming the property of the man who made and laid the snare. The spearing of an elephant, with its enormously thick hide, is no easy matter, as the animal can still make short active rushes. Casualties are not infrequent, and should anyone be caught he is, as a rule, almost certain to be killed.

While the tusk-getting operations were going on I took the opportunity to examine the respective positions of the heart, lungs and brain in relation to the conspicuous points of the animal's exterior, such as the eye, the ear, the line of the fore leg and the point of the shoulder. In order to fix the position of the heart and lungs I made some boys get the stomach and intestines out. This was a terrific job, but we were ably assisted by the powerful native women. The "innards" of elephant are very greatly prized by all natives who eat elephant. The contents of the stomach must have weighed a ton, I should think, and I saw the intestine or sack which contains the clear pure water so readily drunk by the hunter during the dry season when he finds himself far from water. It is from this internal tank that the elephant can produce water for the purpose of treating himself to a shower bath when there is no water. He brings it up into his throat, whence it is sucked into the trunk and then delivered where required. The first time I saw an elephant doing this I thought he must be standing by a pool of water from which he was drawing it. I was many weary miles from water and the sun was scorching, and I and the boy with me were very thirsty, so we hastened towards the elephant, which moved on slowly through the bush. Very soon we arrived at the spot where we had seen him at his shower bath, but no spring or pool could I find. I asked the Karamojan about it and he then told me, with a smile at my ignorance, that the nearest water was at our camp and that all elephant carried water inside them and need not replenish their stock for three days. Coming up with the elephant I killed him and got Pyjalé (my Karamojan tracker) to pierce its water tank, and sure enough water, perfectly clear barring a little blood, gushed out, which we both drank greedily. It was warm certainly, but quite tasteless and odourless and very wholesome and grateful.

When everything had been got out, except the lungs and heart,

I had spears thrust through from the direction from which a bullet would come. I meanwhile peered into the huge cavity formed by the massive ribs and when a spear pierced a lung or the heart, I immediately examined its situation and tried to commit it to my memory. One thing I noticed was that with the animal lying on its side the heart did not occupy the cavity which was obviously intended for it when upright, therefore an allowance had to be made. Another thing I was impressed with was the size of the arteries about the heart. It extended the killing area a considerable distance above the heart, and I have often since killed elephant with a shot above the heart. About the situation of the brain I also learned a lot. I thought I had its position fixed to a nicety in my mind, but I subsequently found that all I had learned was one of the many positions the brain does not occupy. And it was by a series of these misplacings that I finally came to know where the brain really does lie. It is a small object contained in a very large head. It lies so far from the exterior that a very slight and almost unnoticeable change of angle causes the bullet to miss it completely.

From this my first dealing with Karamojans it began to be borne in on me that they were not so bad as the Swahili traders had tried to make out. And my subsequent dealings with them confirmed this impression. As far as I was concerned I had hardly any trouble with them. But at the same time some terrible massacres took place while I was in their country. These affairs were the most completely successful operations I have ever heard of from the native point of view. On three occasions massacres of well armed trading caravans were attempted, and on two there were no survivors among the traders and no casualties among the natives, while on the third there was one trader survivor who escaped. I will describe later on the methods employed by the natives so successfully, for it was not until my Karamojan friend Pyjalé came to me that I heard the inside of the thing. For the next few days nothing of note happened except that we passed the remains of two black men by the roadside—stragglers from some trading caravan probably, judging by the bits of cloth lying about. Now here was a state of things requiring explanation. We were now close to Mani-Mani, the up-country base for all trading caravans. Mani-Mani was also a populous centre for Karamojans, with whom the traders were perforce at peace. And yet here on the roads were two murdered men obviously belonging to the traders. On my arrival at Mani-Mani I found the explanation. It was thus: Among Karamojans, as among Masai, Somals and other tribes, a young man is of no consideration, has no standing with the girls, until he has killed someone. It does not matter how he kills him, he may be asleep or unarmed. When he has " done someone in," either man or woman, other than Karamojan of course, he has the right to tattoo the right side of his body for a man victim and the left side for a woman. Moreover, at the dances he mounts a very tall ostrich feather dipped blood red, and then he is looked upon as a man. He may and does now demand anything from the unmarried girls. He may flog them should they resist. And this atrocious incitement to murder is the cause of death to any legweary straggler from caravans. That the Swahili leaders never made these wayside murders a *casus belli* shows them to be what they are, callous snivellers. That they could have put down this custom was shown when some of my boys lost their way among the villages. As soon as it was reported to me I at once got together five of my askaris and raced off among the herds of Karamojan cattle. We rounded up a huge mob and held them more or less in one place. Spearmen rushed about, women holloaed, and shields were produced from every hut. I was so hot and angry —thinking that the missing boys had been murdered—that I was eager to begin by attacking straightaway. It looked as if about 400 spearmen were assembled and I meant to give them a genuine shaking up with my 10-shot :303, followed by my 10-shot Mauser pistol. I felt confident that as soon as I let loose on them and killed one or two the others would run like rabbits. It never came to a fight, for some old unarmed men and women came tottering up, picking grass at every step, biting it in two and casting the bits to the winds. This meant peace ; peace at any price. Where were my porters? They did not know, really they did not. But they would be all right. Nobody would harm them. I told them to go and produce every one of them unharmed or I would take and kill all their cattle and a lot of them besides. Moreover, if any armed man approached anywhere near to the cattle I would shoot him dead. The cattle would remain there—between ourselves we could not have handled them—until the porters were produced.

And produced they were, very quickly. They had merely lost their way among the villages and had been guided back.

I did not regret having had this opportunity of showing the natives that as far as my people were concerned we were prepared to fight savagely for any member of the safari and not—as did the traders—let stragglers be murdered without even a protest. The noise of this affair travelled far and probably saved us a lot of trouble in our after dealings.

Another reason for this apathy on the part of the Swahili leaders was, I think, that the certainty of murder awaiting anyone on the road prevented desertion. They were enabled by this means to keep their boys for years without payment of wages. So long as they could prevent the boys from reaching Mumias alive there was no redress. Hence it was difficult for the Government representative at Mumias to get reliable information of the internal state of Karamojo.

On our arrival at Mani-Mani we were met by one Shundi—a remarkable man. Kavirondo by birth, he had been captured early in life, taken to the coast and sold as a slave. Being a man of great force of character he had soon freed himself by turning Mohammedan. Thence onward fortune had smiled upon him until at last here he was, the recognised chief *Tajir* (rich man) of all the traders. Having naturally the intelligence to recognise the value of bluff and from his primitive ancestors the nerve to carry it off, he was at this time the greatest of all the traders. Just as he had been a leader while slave-raiding was the order of the day, so now he led when ivory had given place to slaves as a commodity. One other thing makes him conspicuous, at any rate, in my mind, and that was the fact that he had owned the slave who had laid low the elephant which bore the enormous tusks, one of which now reposes in the South Kensington Museum. These tusks are still, as far as I know, the record. The one which we have in London scales 234 lb. or thereabouts. According to Shundi his slave killed it with a muzzle-loader on the slopes of Kilimandjaro.

Shundi was accompanied by a large body of traders of all sorts. There were Arabs, Swahilis, one or two Persians and a few African born Baluchis, and a pretty tough lot they looked. Beside their mean and cunning air Shundi—the great coal-black Bantu—appeared like a lion among hyenas. What an extraordinary calm and dignity some of these outstanding black men have. Here was a kin spirit to Buba Gida.

They hated my appearing in their country, but did not show it. Shundi took it in the spirit that what had to be had to be, but some of the lesser villains were obviously nervous. They pretended to wish me to camp inside the town, but I preferred to remain outside. The town was of very considerable size, although the buildings were of a temporary construction. I remarked an extraordinary number of women about and thought that I recognised Masai types among them. This was so, as I afterwards learnt that Shundi alone had over eighty women, many of whom were Masai from Kilimandjaro.

With native politeness gifts of food, etc., were offered and presently all withdrew, intimating that they would return when I had rested.

They must have been feeling rather uncomfortable about the appearance in their midst of a white man, possibly an agent of that detestable Government so troublesome about raiding. I did not actually know at the time, but learnt afterwards that at the very moment of my arrival in their midst they had an enormous raid on the Turkana underway.

In the afternoon they came again and we had the usual ceremonial palaver. Every one was strictly guarded, but they made a distinct effort to embroil me with the natives in the hope, I suppose, of getting me so mixed up in some shooting affair that I would become more or less one of themselves. I refused to have anything to do with their intrigues. I got little information regarding elephant from these people. In fact, neither side could quite overcome a severely suppressed but quite strong hostility to the other.

I stayed a few days at Mani-Mani as there were repairs to be attended to and man and beast required a rest. The first sign of trouble soon appeared, caused, I feel certain, by Swahili intrigue. It was the dry season and all animals were watered once a day at the wells dug in the otherwise dry river-bed. My animals were being watered as usual. That is, water was drawn from the well in buckets and emptied into a watertight ground sheet laid over a suitable depression in the sand. Word was suddenly brought to me that the natives refused to allow my animals to be watered. I went at once to the scene and asked the natives what all the trouble was about. There were about forty young bloods leaning against their spears and they laughed in the most insolent manner without giving me any answer. I turned to my herds and beckoned them to bring up the animals. As they began to do so three of the bloods strode over and began flogging the thirsty bullocks in the face and driving them off. It was now or never, first impression and so on. I seized from the nearest Karamojan his cutting-edged club, sprang over to one of the bullock obstructors and dealt him the hardest blow on the head I possibly could. I was fairly hefty, in good training, and meant all I knew. To my astonishment the native turned on me a smile instead of dropping dead or at least stunned, while the club flew to atoms. I had hit his shock-absorbing periwig, previously described. I might as well have hit a Dunlop Magnum.

I must confess it was rather a set-back. However, one good effect it had was that everyone, except myself, roared with laughter, and then when even I began to see the humour of it I spotted a mischievous devil calmly jabbing his spear through our priceless waterproof ground sheet. This would not do, so I drew my Mauser pistol. Now these natives were then at a most dangerous stage of ignorance with regard to firearms. Their experience of them had been gathered on raids with the Swahilis, and they all firmly held the conviction that all you had to do to avoid being struck by the bullet was to *duck when you saw the smoke*. While I was fitting the wooden holster to the Mauser they watched me carefully. They had probably never seen such a gun before if they even recognised it as such. When therefore I had it fitted up and was covering them no one moved. They were waiting, I suspect, for the smoke. And when they heard the particularly vicious bang of the little Mauser and saw no smoke, the laugh this time was rather on them, and especially on the gentleman who had been so busy with his spear and my ground sheet; for he now stood looking at a half severed and completely spoilt spear in his hand with a ridiculous air of surprised injury. In a few seconds the humour of this phase struck all concerned, although the natives began to edge nervously away. All their swagger was gone now. I had been approaching the fellow with the damaged spear, and now suddenly set upon him, relying upon my herds to help me. Never have I felt anything like the sinewy strength of that greasy native; he was all but off when the boys secured him just in time. Seeing some flourishing of spears going on among the others, I began pasting dust about them with the little Mauser. Seeing no smoke again, yet getting whing whang right and left of them, they turned and bolted. I got in another clip of ten and kept them dodging dust-bursts for 400 or 500 yds.

On returning I put it out among the natives that our prisoner would be released when ten goats and sheep had been paid by his family as a fine. They were soon forthcoming.

Up till now I had been looked upon by the natives as a sort of poor Arab. In this idea they were no doubt helped by the traders. They had never seen white men, and they saw my mean little safari and drew their own conclusions from appearances. But after the affair at the water hole I was treated with much greater respect, and with a kind of good-humoured indulgence, much as a very persistent headstrong child might be looked upon. And eventually, after a few more " incidents," we became fast friends and they would do almost anything for me or for my people. One instance of this I may as well here record, although it happened long afterwards.

Away down in civilised parts I had left two aged Wanyamwezi boys in charge of my cattle ranch. This was situated a few miles from Nandi Boma (Government Post). At the Boma post office I had left directions for my letters to be forwarded to another Boma on the slopes of Elgon, where I used to send every six months or so to get them. All my letters went as directed until there occurred a change of District Commissioner. Now one of my old pensioners looking after the ranch had orders to report every fortnight to the D.C. that all was well or otherwise. In pursuit of these instructions the old boy appeared one day before the new D.C., who asked him who he was. He said he belonged to me, naming me. The D.C. said he had some letters for me, and told the boy to *take them to me*, thinking that I was at the ranch a few miles off, instead of which I was actually over 600 miles away. That dear old man took the letters without a word, went straight back to the ranch and prepared to follow me into what was much of it quite unknown country. He told the other boy, who was also about sixty-five years of age, that he would have to look after everything himself as he was going after the Bwana (master). Being a thrifty old soul, he had by him much stock of dry smoked beef from cows which had died. His preparations were, therefore, almost complete. An inveterate snuff-taker, he had only to grind up a good quantity for the journey and he was ready. Shouldering his

Snider and with the packet of letters cunningly guarded against wet, off he set through the wilderness, steering due north. Sleeping by night alone by his camp fire and travelling the whole of the day, he came wandering through what would have been to anyone else hostile tribe after hostile tribe. Countries where if I sent at all I sent at least five guns as escort he came through without trouble. How often he must have been looked upon by the lecherous eyes of would-be bloods as fair game for their spears and as means of gaining the coveted tattoo marks and the blood red ostrich feather. But so sublimely unconscious was he of any feeling of nervousness and so bold and confident his bearing that nothing happened. Being old and wise, he courted the routes which led through the most populous centres instead of dodging along the neutral zones between tribes as a nervous man would have done. Had he done this he would to a certainty have been killed. Wherever he went he slept in the largest village, demanded *and got* the best of everything, and eventually reached me intact. It was a splendid effort. He walked into camp as if he had left it five minutes before, and he still had smoked beef and snuff when he arrived. The dear old hoarder had lived to some purpose on the natives as he passed through. He arrived, if you please, escorted by a number of Karamojan big-men, this dingy and, I have to say it, very dirty old man. The letters, alas! proved to be most uninteresting in themselves, but, nevertheless, they formed a link with civilisation. They were chiefly bills from unscrupulous Coast merchants being rendered for the third and fourth time although already paid at least once.

The newspapers were, of course, very old, but produced an extraordinary feeling of uneasiness or disquietude. Leading the life I then was, with its freedom from financial care—money was valueless and never handled—from responsibility—there was no law in the land except that of force—it had rather the effect of a sudden chill to read of strikes, famines, railway accidents, unemployment, lawsuits, and the other thousand and one unhappinesses usually contained in newspapers. Although I read them, every word, including the advertisements—here again remedies for ills— I felt distinctly perturbed for two or three days after. The happiest literature I ever had in the bush was "Pickwick Papers," and the happiest newspaper the dear old *Field*.

III.—The Coming of Pyjalé

From Mani-Mani we moved on to Bukora, another section of Karamojans. I was warned by the Swahilis that Bukora was a very bad country. The people were very rich in cattle and correspondingly insolent. Everyone who passed through Bukora had trouble. Either stock was stolen or porters murdered.

I cannot say that I believed all this, or perhaps I would not have been so ready to go there. But that there was some truth in their statements I soon found. In fact, there were moments when it was touch and go. Looking back on it calmly I can see that nothing but chance luck saved us. It was thus: We pushed our way smartly right into the middle of Bukora, intending to camp near some large village. But to our disappointment the catchments of water were nearly dry. What remained in them was merely mud. We were obliged therefore to move on to some wells on the outskirts of the villages. This is always a bad place to be attacked in. Natives are much more willing to attack people outside than when they are right in their midst. When you are close alongside a village and there is any question of hostilities, the people of that particular village feel that they will probably come in for more than their share of the trouble when it begins. They have their goods and chattels there, their corn, cows, babies, fowls, etc. For these reasons they are against hostilities. Another advantage to the travellers when close to stockaded villages—as these were— is that such a village can be rushed and then held against the rest of the tribe.

However, I was young and without much thought of anything

in those days, and camp by the wells I would. We accordingly did so. And presently the camp began to fill with apparently friendly natives. They dropped in by twos and threes and stood around, each man with two spears. I thought they seemed a nice friendly, sociable crowd, and took little further heed of them. Then comes my headman, a Swahili, to me. "Bwana, there is no good brewing. These people mean trouble. Look around, do you see a single woman anywhere?" I laughed and asked him what he thought they would do. He said that at a given pre-arranged signal they would start spearing everyone. And then it dawned on me how absurdly easy it would be for them to do so. When you came to look around with this thought in your mind it became apparent that every man was being marked by several spearmen. If he moved they also lounged about until they were again close to him. I must say they appeared to me to act the indifference part very well. When I had convinced myself that something of this nature really was afoot, I naturally got close to my shooting irons, ready to take a hand when the fun started. In those days I always wore fifty rounds in my belt.

Now I thought that if I could only supply something sufficiently distracting the affair might never begin. There over the plains were plenty of game. I took my rifle and got the interpreter to tell the Karamojans to come as I was going killing meat. They came at once in fair numbers. They had already heard of my wonderful rifles, and wherever I went I always had an audience eager to see them or the Bom-bom (Mauser pistol) at work.

Hardly had we gone a few hundred yards, and while we were still in full view of the camp, when a herd of zebra came galloping across our front. They had been alarmed by some abnormal movement of natives and had somehow got mixed up and lost.

They came well spaced apart and just right for my purpose. I shot one after the other as hard as I could fire. I was using a 10 shot ·303, and when I had fired the ten shots the survivors of the herd were too far off. I was careful not to reload in the ordinary way, for I carried another charged magazine. Consequently the natives thought I might have any number of shots left in this quite new and terrifying weapon. No smoke and such a rapid fire of death—they had never seen the like. Bing! bing! bing! bing! bing! they kept saying to themselves, only much more rapidly than the actual rate of fire. And the zebras, strong brutes, knocked right down one after the other. No! this was something new. They had better be careful about fooling around with this *red* man. He was different from those red men among the Swahilis, who used to fire great clouds of smoke and hit nothing.

After an episode of this kind one *feels* somehow that a complete mental transformation has taken place. One is established right above these, in some ways, finer but less scientific people. But this knowledge comes to both at the same time. I now ordered these previously truculent, now almost servile, savages to flay, cut up and carry to camp every bit of meat and skin. When I saw anyone sneaking a bit of fat or what-not I blackguarded him soundly. I rushed the whole regiment back to camp loaded with several tons of meat, many of them forgetting their spears in their hurry. But had I ventured to bullyrag them like this before the zebra incident I would have had a spear thrust for answer and right quickly too.

I now began to push enquiries about elephant, but with no great success at first. One day a Bukora boy came to camp and while in conversation with some of my people casually told them that he had recently returned from no man's land, where he and some friends of his had been looking for Kumamma. The Kumamma were their neighbours to the west. They had been looking for them in order to spear them, should things be right — that meaning should the enemy be in sufficiently small force for them to easily overcome. When the numbers are at all equal, both sides retire smartly to the rear. This is the normal kind of state in which these tribes live. It leads to a few deaths certainly, but it keeps the young men fit and out of other mischief. Every young man goes looking for blood frequently, and as they carry no food except a few handfuls of unground millet simply soaked in water, and as they never dare to sleep while in the neutral zone, it acts as a kind of field training.

This youth, then, had seen no Kumamma but had seen elephant. My boys told me this and I tried to get the lad to go with us to hunt. He said he would come back and let me know. He did so and brought a friend. This friend of his was a most remarkable-looking man. Strange as it may seem, he had a most intellectual head. He was a man of perhaps thirty-five years of age, most beautifully made and tattooed for men victims only, I was relieved to see. Pyjalé was his name, and now began a firm and long friendship between this distinguished savage and myself. I cannot say that I have ever had the same feelings for any man as I came to have for Pyjalé. He was, I found, a thorough man, courageous, quiet, modest, with a horror of humbug and untiring in our common pact, the pursuit of elephant. He was with me during the greater part of my time in Karamojo, and although surrounded by people who clothed themselves, never would he wear a rag even. Nor would he sleep comfortably as we did on grass and blankets. The bare hard ground out by the camp fire with a hole dug for his hip bone and his little wooden pillow had been good enough for him before and was good enough now. No one poked fun at Pyjalé for his nakedness; he was the kind who do not get fun poked at them.

Pyjalé was game to show us elephants, but said we would have to travel far. His intelligence was at once apparent by his saying that we ought to take tents as the rains might come any day. He was right, for come they did while we were hunting.

I took to Pyjalé right at the start and asked him what I should do about the main safari. He said I could leave it where it was; no one would interfere with it. If I liked I could leave the ivory in one of the villages. This I gathered was equivalent to putting one's silver in the bank at home. And so it is, bizarre as it may seem. You may leave anything with natives—ivory, beads, which are money, trade goods, stock, anything—and not one thing will they take provided you place it in their care. But if you leave your own people to look after it they will steal it, given the chance.

Thinking that it might save trouble I put all my trade goods and ivory in a village, and leaving the safari with plenty of rations, I left for a few days' hunting, taking a sufficient number of porters to bring home any ivory we were likely to get. This was necessary at this time as the natives did not yet follow me in hundreds wherever I went, as they did later on.

We trekked hard for three days and came once more in sight of the Debasien range, but on its other side. On the night of the third day the rains burst upon us. The light calico bush tents were hastily erected in a perfect gale and downpour. Even Pyjalé had to shelter.

In the morning Pyjalé said we were certain to see elephant if we could only cross a river which lay ahead of us. When we reached its banks it was a raging torrent, red with mud and covered with patches of white froth. There was nothing for it but to camp and wait until the spate subsided.

While this was being done I saw a snake being carried down by the swollen river. Then I saw another and another. Evidently banks were being washed away somewhere.

A boy pointed to my shorts and said that a *doodoo* (insect) had crawled up the inside of one of my legs. Thinking, perhaps, it was a fly, or not thinking at all, perhaps, I slapped my leg hard with open hand and got a most frightful sting, while a huge scorpion dropped half crushed to the ground. But not before he had injected quite sufficient poison into me. "Insect," indeed! how I cursed that boy. And then, by way of helping me, he said that when people were stung by these big black scorpions—like mine— they always died. He was in a frightful state. And then another fool boy said : " Yes, no one ever recovered from that kind." I shouted for whisky, for you certainly could feel the poison going through the circulation. I knew that what the boys said was bunkum, but still I drank a lot of whisky. My leg swelled and I could not sleep that night, but I was quite all right next day.

The river had gone down somewhat, so I proposed to cross. No one was very eager to go across with a rope. A rope was necessary, as some of the boys could not swim and the current was running too strong for them to walk across the bottom under water, carrying stones to keep them down, as they usually did.

I carried at that time a Mexican raw hide lariat and thought that this stretched across would do nicely for the boys to haul themselves over by. So I took one end to the other side and made it fast, when the safari began to come over. Once the plunge had been taken I found that more of them could swim than they had led me to believe. Then the inevitable—when raw hide gets wet—happened and the rope parted. As luck would have it there was a boy about mid-stream at the instant. The slippery end slid through his fingers and he went rapidly down-stream. His head kept going under and reappearing I noticed, but thought that, as he had a smile on his face each time he came up, he was another humbug pretending to be unable to swim. His friends, who knew perfectly well that he could not swim a yard, said, of course, not a word. And it was not until he gushed water at the mouth instead of air that I realised he was drowning. I ran down the bank while another boy plunged in at the crossing place. I reached the boy first by a second and we soon had him towing to bank. Black men are good to save, they never seem to realise their close call and do not clutch and try to climb out on you. While towing to the bank I felt something on my head and put up a hand to brush it off. Horrors, a snake! It was merely trying to save itself on anything above water level, but I did not realise this. Whenever I knocked it off it seemed to come again. Luckily we just then reached the bank or in another instant I would have abandoned my drowning porter to save myself from that beastly serpent. It was all very silly, and the snake was nearly at its last gasp, but I did not see the humour at the moment.   Needless to say, the boy was perfectly all right in ten minutes after vomiting up a bucket or two of water.

While we were getting ready again for the march we heard elephant.   To my inexperienced ear the sound seemed to come from some bush 400 yds. or 500 yds. away.   But Pyjalé said, to my astonishment, that they were a long way off and that unless we hurried we should not see them before sundown.   As the sun then indicated about one o'clock, I thought he was wrong.   But he was not; for it was half an hour from sunset when we saw them, still far away.   I remember looking industriously about all those miles expecting momentarily to see elephant, while Pyjalé soaked along ahead of me without a glance aside.   The only explanation of this extraordinary sound-carrying that has ever occurred to me is humidity of atmosphere.   During the dry season the earth becomes so hot that when the first rains fall much is evaporated in steam and the humidity is remarkable.

Here we were face to face with such a gathering of elephant as I had never dared to dream of even.   The whole country was black with them, and what lay beyond them one could not see as the country was dead flat.   Some of them were up to their knees in water, and when we reached their tracks the going became very bad.   The water was so opaque with mud as to quite hide the huge pot-holes made by the heavy animals.   You were in and out the whole time.   As we drew nearer I thought that we ought to go decently and quietly, at any rate make some pretence of stalking them, if only out of respect to them.   But no, that awful Pyjalé rushed me, splashing and squelching right up to them.   He was awfully good, and I began to learn a lot from him.   He treated elephant with complete indifference.   If he were moved at all, and that was seldom, he would smile.

I was for treating them as dangerous animals, especially when we trod on the heels of small bogged-down calves and their mothers came rushing back at us in the most alarming fashion, but Pyjalé would have none of it. Up to the big bulls would he have me go, even if we had to go under infuriated cows. He made me kill seven before sundown stopped the bloodshed.

With great difficulty we found a spot a little higher than the surrounding country and fairly dry. As usual at these flood times the little island was crawling with ants of every description. How comes it that ants do not drown, although they cannot swim? They appear to be covered with something which repels water.

Scorpions and all kinds of other horrors were there also. One of the boys was bitten and made a fearful fuss all night about it.

I expected to do well on the morrow, but when it came, behold, not an elephant in sight. Such are the surprises of elephant hunting. Yesterday when light failed hundreds upon hundreds in sight and now an empty wilderness.

We had not alarmed them, as I noticed that when a shot was fired only the animals in the vicinity ran and that for a short distance only. There were too many to stampede even had they been familiar with firearms. And the noise was such as to drown the crack of a ·303 almost immediately.

I asked Pyjalé what he thought about it. He said that at the beginning of the rains elephant wandered all over the country. You could never tell where they might be. With water and mud and green food springing up everywhere they were under no necessity to frequent any one district more than another. Pyjalé's advice was to get the ivory out and take it home, and then he would show me a country where we were certain to get big bulls. Accordingly the boys set about chopping out while I went for a cruise around to make certain there was nothing about.

I saw nothing but ostrich, giraffe and great herds of common and Topi haartebeeste. On crossing some black-cotton soil I noticed that it clung to the boots in a very tiresome way. Each time you lifted a foot, 10 lb. or 15 lb. of sticky mud came with it. At this stage the ground was still dry underneath, only the top few inches being wet. From the big lumps lying about where antelope had passed it was obvious that they had, too, the same trouble as I was having, *i.e.*, mud clinging to the feet.

But on watching Pyjalé it appeared that it did not stick to naked human feet to anything like the same extent. Pyjalé told me, and I afterwards saw it actually done, that it was possible to run down ostrich and the heavy antelope, such as eland, when the ground was in this state.

Returning we found the boys well on with their chopping out. Towards evening we started for home, being much troubled with swollen rivers. Most of the boys walked through the rivers when we could find a place where the current was not too strong. The heavy tusks, of course, kept them on the bottom. But it was a curious sight to see them calmly marching in deeper and deeper until their heads went right under, reappearing again close to the other bank. Of course, the distance they thus traversed was only a few yards, but for fellows who cannot swim it was not bad.

One camp from home (the safari) we slept near some flooded wells. The boys took their tusks to scrub them with sand and water, the better to make an appearance on the morrow when we should rejoin the safari. This is always a source of joy to Wanyamwezi, to carry ivory to the base. When allowed to do so they will spend hours dancing and singing their way into the camp. The women turn out, everybody makes a noise of some kind, from blowing a reed pipe, to trumpeting on a water buck horn or beating a drum or a tin, in fact anything so that it produces noise.

While they were scrubbing the tusks one of these slipped from the boy's hands into a well. I heard of it and went to see what could be done. To test the depth I tried one of Pyjalé's 9 ft. spears. No good. Then I tied another to it, but even then I could not touch bottom. Pyjalé said the bottom was very far. Then I looked at one of my boys squatting on the edge of the well. He had been a coast canoe-man shark-fisher—than whom no finer watermen exist—and knew what I meant without a word passing. He tied his cloth between his legs and stripped his upper body. Then jumping into the air he twisted half round and went down head first into the very middle of the well. It seemed ages before his head reappeared. At last it did so, but only for an instant. Down again; apparently he had not found it the first time. After another long wait he came up with the tusk and swimming or treading water. Eager hands clutched the tusk and drew it out, the boy crawled out himself. This particular tusk weighed 65 lb., the length being almost the diameter of the well, so it had to be brought up end on. How he did it I cannot imagine. The water was the colour of pea-soup, and a scrubbed tusk is like a greasy pole to hold. Of course, it would not weigh 65 lb. when submerged, but it was a pretty good effort I thought. I know I would not have gone 20 ft. or 30 ft. down that well for any number of tusks.

These boys have the most extraordinary lungs. I once sent one of them down to disentangle the anchor of a motor launch, which had got foul of something. There were about four fathoms of chain and the boy went down this hand over hand. I only wanted him to clear the anchor, when we would heave it up in the ordinary way. But presently up the chain came the boy and the anchor.

On the morrow we entered Bukora again, with fourteen fine white tusks. We had a great reception at our camp. The natives, too, were rather astonished at our rapid success. Pyjalé stalked along without any show of feeling.

The boys who had stayed behind had nothing to report except the loss of three of our sheep by theft. Now it was essential to nip this kind of thing in the bud. I did nothing that day, merely sending Pyjalé to his home with a handsome present. I knew he would put it round as to the kind of people we were. Natives always exaggerate enormously when back from a scurry in the bush, and his account of our doings would probably have made me blush had I heard it.

Next day when Pyjalé came with a pot of fresh cow's milk as a present, I asked him if he had heard anything about our sheep. He said no. I asked him to point me out the village which had stolen them. He said they would kill him if he did so. Therefore he knew. I then said that he need not go with me, if only he would indicate it. He said the village with the three tamarind trees was where the thieves lived.

I went over quietly, as if looking for guinea-fowl, in the evening. The village was quite close to our camp. When their stock began to come in I signalled up some boys. We walked up deliberately to the herds, no one taking any great notice of us. I separated out a mob of sheep and goats and we started driving them towards camp, but very quietly and calmly. It is wonderful how imitative Africans are. If you are excited they at once become so. If you are calm and deliberate, so are they.

A more dramatic thing would have been to take the cattle. But these native cattle are not used to boys wearing clothes, as mine did, and we found at Mani-Mani that they became excited and difficult to handle unless they see their black naked owners about. Pyjalé I had carefully left out of this business.

As soon as our object dawned upon the Karamojans there was the usual commotion. Women wha! wha! wha-ed while rushing from the huts with shields; warriors seized these and rushed with prodigious speed directly away from us; while we pushed our two or three hundred hostages slowly along.

Arrived at camp we just managed to squeeze them all into the bullock boma. There were noises all round us now. The boys were uneasy; there is always something in the alarm note when issued by hundreds of human throats. Dark was soon on us and we sat up by the camp fires till fairly late. Nothing happened, as I anticipated. Discretion had won. They hated that little bom-bom so.

What I wanted now was that they should come. I wanted to tell them why I had taken their sheep. No one appeared, but I consoled myself with the thought that they jolly well knew why I had taken them.

Presently there appeared to be great signs of activity in one of the nearer villages. Native men kept coming from all directions. My boys were all eyes for this, to them, impending attack. I thought they must be born fools to try anything of that sort in broad daylight. Night was their best chance.

Pyjalé had been absent, so I hoped that he was at the meeting. Presently he appeared. He said they had had a discussion and had concluded not to attack us. I told him to go straight back and invite them all to come; I wanted to be attacked. And moreover, if my sheep were not instantly brought I would proceed to kill the hostage sheep we held, and that then I would proceed to hunt the thieves.

This acted like magic; I suppose they thought that as I had known the village of the thieves, I also probably knew the actual men themselves. Our sheep were very soon brought and the hostages released.

I took the opportunity when the natives were there to impress upon them that we did not want anything from them. All we wanted was to hunt elephant in peace, but at the same time I hinted that we could be very terrible indeed. I got some of the older men to dry up and sit down, in a friendly way, and we had a good talk together. I now brought out the card to which I owed all my success in killing elephant in Karamojo. I offered a cow as reward for information leading to my killing five or more bull elephant. This was an unheard of reward. There a cow of breeding age is simply priceless. Normally natives never kill or sell she-stock of any kind and cows could only be obtained by successful raiding. Now among Africans there are numbers of young men who just lack the quality which brings success to its lucky owner, just as there are in every community, and to these young men my offer appealed tremendously. That they believed in my promise from the very start was, I thought, a great compliment, not only to me, but to their astuteness in perceiving that there was a difference between white men and Swahilis.

When my offer had gone the rounds the whole country for many miles round was scoured for elephant, with the result that I never could have a day's rest. Everyone was looking for elephant. But had the reward been trade goods scarcely a soul would have bothered about it.

The first man to come was remarkable looking enough to satisfy anybody. A terrible looking man. A grotesquely hideous face above a very broad and deep chest, all mounted on the spindliest of knock-kneed legs. Chest, arms, shoulders, stomach and back heavily tattooed, denoting much killing. By reputation a terrific fighter, and very wealthy.

At first I thought that he was come to show me elephant. That was his intention, he said, but first he wanted to become my blood-brother. He said he could see that I was a kindred spirit and that we two should be friends. He said he had no friends. How was that? I asked. Pyjalé answered in a whisper that the lion never made friends of jackals and hyenas. And so we became friends. I was not going through the blood-brotherhood business, with its eating of bits of toasted meat smeared with each other's blood, sawing in two of living dogs or nonsense of that kind. I took his hand and wrung it hard, and had it explained to him that among us that was an extraordinarily potent way of doing it. That seemed to satisfy the old boy, for the act of shaking hands was as strange to him as the act of eating each other's blood is to us.

He started off then and I said : " What about those elephant?" " Wait," was the answer, and off he went, to return shortly with a fat bullock. And then I found that my friend was the wealthiest cattle owner anywhere about—a kind of multi-millionaire. I thought to myself, well, he will not look for elephant. Nor did he ; but he had sons without number, being much married, whom he scattered far and wide to look for them. He had arranged the thing most perfectly. We went with food for a few days and returned laden with ivory. Besides which we had some of the jolliest nights in the bush.

This great man being now my friend, our troubles were at an end. Wherever we went we were followed by scores of the young unmarried girls and one old maid—the only one I have come across in Karamojo. She was so outstandingly above the average in good looks, so beautifully made and so obviously still quite young, that I often asked why she should remain a spinster. They told me that no man would marry her because she was so beautiful. But why should that be a bar? we white men like our wives to be beautiful. They thought this strange, even for white men. They said they never married very beautiful women as all men wanted them. They also gave as another reason that these very attractive women wanted all men. And I must say that our camp beauty gave decided colour to this latter statement.

No sooner were we arrived back with our imposing line of beautiful tusks than other natives clamoured to take us to elephant. They wanted me to go there and then, but I needed a rest.

In the evening I presented my friend with a heifer, when to my astonishment he refused it. He said he wanted nothing from his friend. I was rather suspicious about this at first, but I need not have been, as I subsequently found this man to be thoroughly genuine. I am convinced that he would have given me anything. It is a big affair in their lives, this blood-brotherhood. Apparently we now owned everything in common. He offered me any of his daughters in marriage, and, thank goodness, never asked me for my rifle. From now on he followed me about like a faithful dog, some of his young wives attending to his commissariat arrangements wherever he was. He even took my name, which was Longelly-nyung or Red Man. And he began now to call his young male children, of whom he was very fond, by the same name. He was a delightfully simple fellow at heart and as courageous as a lion, as I had proof later.

After a few more journeys to the bush lasting from four to

ten days, I found suddenly that I had as much ivory as I could possibly move.   And this, while still on the fringe of Karamojo. I decided to return to Mumias, sell my ivory, fit out a real good expedition capable of moving several tons of ivory, and return to Karamojo fitted out for several years in the bush.

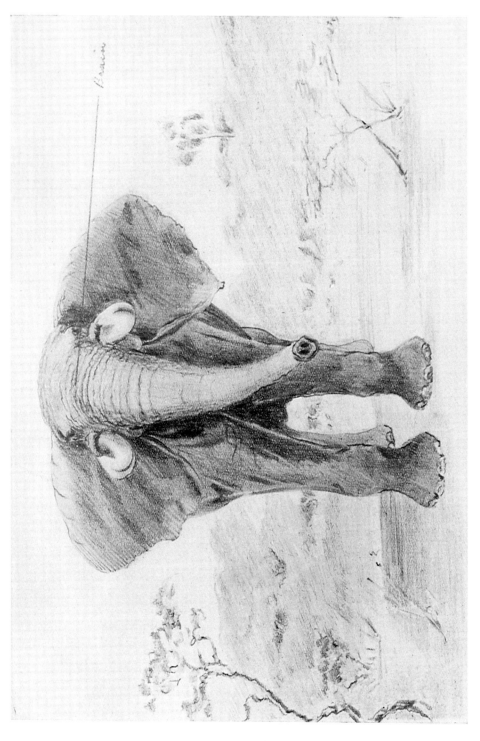

THE DEADLIEST AND MOST HUMANE METHOD OF KILLING THE AFRICAN ELEPHANT IS THE SHOT IN THE
COMPARATIVELY SMALL BRAIN CONTAINED IN HIS GIGANTIC HEAD.

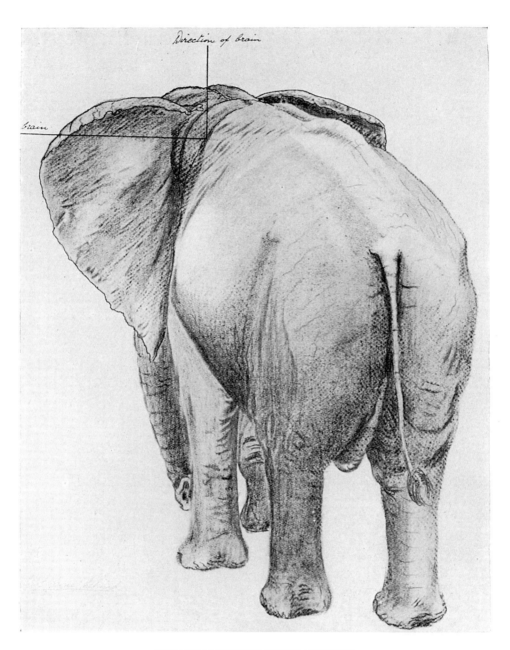

Direction of brain

brain

THE BRAIN SHOT FROM BEHIND

THE FALLING SPEAR: THE DEADLIEST NATIVE ELEPHANT TRAP

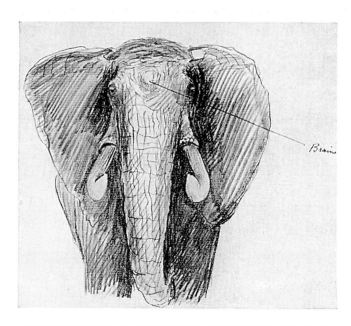

THE POSITION OF THE BRAIN WHEN THE HEAD IS
VIEWED FROM THE FRONT

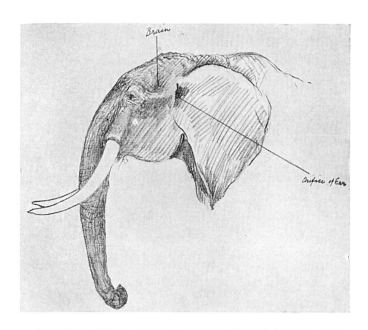

LOCATING THE BRAIN WITH THE SIDE OF THE HEAD
TO THE SPORTSMAN

THE MARAUDING BULL

THE ELEPHANT, AFTER THE BRAIN SHOT, DIES QUIETLY AND THE
OTHERS DO NOT TAKE ALARM.

THE ANGRY BULL

A magnificent sight but extremely difficult to deal with

WHERE THE WINDPIPE ENTERS THE BODY IS THE SPOT TO HIT WHEN THE ANIMAL IS IN THIS POSITION.

ELEPHANT IN THE COUNTRY MOST SUITED TO THE BODY SHOT
Even here, on an open grassy plain, if the hunter can get within thirty or forty yards, the brain shot is to be preferred.

WITH THE HERD IN THE PAIRING SEASON

WITH ONE EYE SHUT
The shaded portion represents the hands holding the rifle.

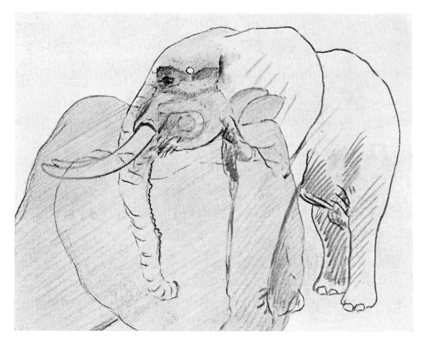

WITH BOTH EYES OPEN
The whole of the head is visible through the hands and rifle.

THE DOTTED LINES SHOW THE POSITION OF THE HEART AND LUNGS.

ELEPHANT SLINKING AWAY, WARNED OF THE APPROACH OF MAN BY HONEY-GUIDES

MEDICINE INDEED!

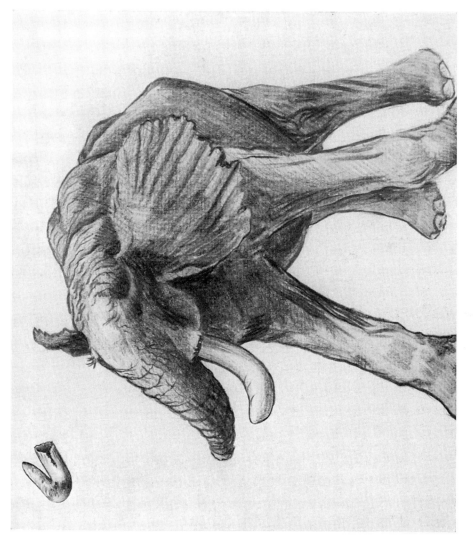

HE SHOOK HIS HEAD SO VIOLENTLY IN THE DEATH THROES THAT A TUSK FLEW OUT AND LANDED TWELVE PACES AWAY.

A M'BONI VILLAGE

Perhaps twenty grass shelters are dotted here and there under the trees.

A PATRIARCH

"A SMALL NATIVE BOY WAS IN THE ACT OF PINKING AN ENORMOUS ELEPHANT."

POOR KARAMOJANS, SHOWING PERIWIGS

CARRYING THE IVORY

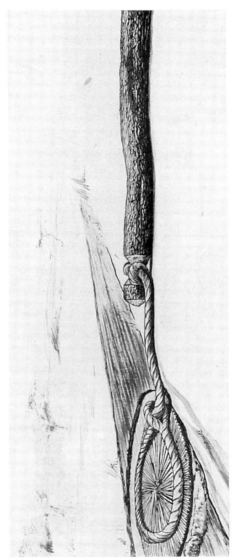

ELEPHANT SNARE NET SET, BUT NOT YET COVERED

KARAMOJAN WARRIOR

After a warrior has killed anyone, he is entitled to wear a white ostrich feather dipped in blood-red, and tattoo himself on the right side if the slain was a man and the left if a woman.

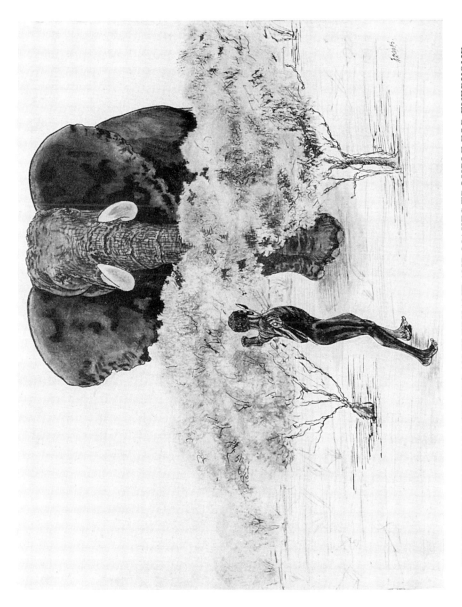

THAT LUNATIC PYJALE SPEARS AN ELEPHANT AND MAKES TROUBLE FOR EVERYONE.

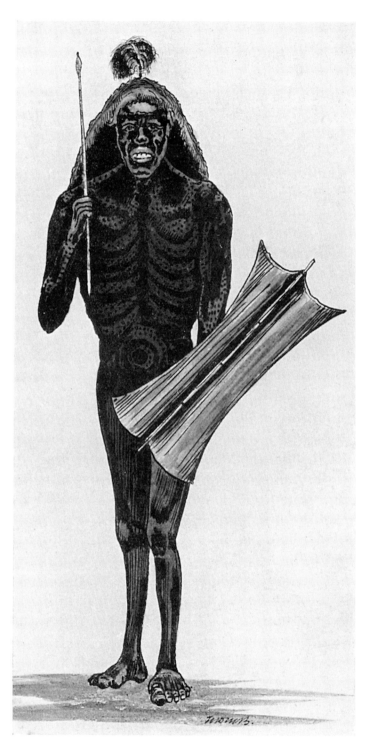

LONGELLY-NYMUNG, THE AUTHOR'S BLOOD BROTHER
One of the best spear-fighters and therefore wealthy in cattle. He was an exceptional man, would accept no gifts, but took Mr. Bell's native name and also called his male children by it.

THE RETURN OF THE SAFARI

"THE ELEPHANT NEARLY FELL OVER WITH FRIGHT: HIS TRUNK SHOT OUT; HIS EARS LOOKED LIKE UMBRELLAS TURNED INSIDE OUT."

Watching the Northern Trail

WATCHING THE NORTHERN TRAIL FOR THE RETURNING RAIDERS

LOOKING INTO THE BRILLIANTLY LIT OPEN SPACE FROM THE TWILIGHT OF
THE FOREST

ABYSSINIAN SLAVERS

FROM THE LOOK-OUT HILL

"The next morning I climbed the little hill in pouring rain. From its top I had a good view of the Murua to the south, while to the north a river was visible flowing northwards. On its banks were large verdant green flats which might have been as smooth as tennis lawns but for the fact that they were thickly speckled with black dots which the glasses and then the telescope showed to be the backs and heads of scores of bull elephants."

SULIEMANI BUMPS INTO HIS BULL

THE CAMP CHRONICLER

A SHOT FROM THE SHOULDERS OF A TALL NATIVE: A VERY WOBBLY METHOD

TELESCOPE TRIPOD AS STAND IN HIGH GRASS

ELEPHANT IN THE UPPER NILE SWAMP

IN THE LADO ENCLAVE: WHITE RHINO, LION, AND ELEPHANT

VI

DABOSSA

HAVING now the wherewithal to fit out a real good safari from the sale of my ivory, I proceeded to discharge my Baganda porters and to engage in their place Wanyamweze. Bagandas being banana-eaters had shown themselves to be good lads enough, but poor "doers" on ground millet, flour and elephant meat. Dysentery was their trouble. Whereas Wanyamweze seemed capable of keeping their condition indefinitely under severe safari conditions. All my former boys had a good pay-day coming to them, as, of course, they had been unable to spend anything while in Karamojo. Consequently they one and all went on the burst. A few new clothes from the Indian shops and the rest on native beer was the rule. When drinking largely of native beer no other food is required as the whole grain is contained in it. My two Nandi cowherds spent hardly anything of their wages. The only things I ever saw them buy were a fat sheep and two tins of sweet condensed milk. They rendered down about two quarts of fat from the tail of the sheep, poured in the contents of the milk tins, stirred it well and drank it off.

This time bullocks were not employed, donkeys taking their place. It was in connection with the buying of these donkeys that a remarkable feat of foot-travelling came to my notice. A trader wished to sell to me some donkeys—probably raided—which he had left at Mani-Mani, about 150 miles away. He offered a Karamojan a cow as reward for bringing them down in time for me to buy, and the boy had them there at the end of the fourth day. As nearly as I could ascertain he had covered 300 miles in 100 hours.

We crossed the Turkwell about 102 strong, this number not including women and camp followers. At Mani-Mani and Bukora some of our cows were exchanged for sheep, goats and donkeys. A decent cow would bring sixty sheep or goats. A donkey was the equivalent of ten sheep or goats. Having now so many mouths to feed it was necessary to buy many donkeys. I raised our donkey strength to 160. This meant that I could have constantly loaded about eighty. They were chiefly employed in carrying grain to our base camp in Dodose, sometimes from Mt. Elgon, where banana flour could be got, over 200 miles away, or from the country near the Nile, 150 to 200 miles distant. Throughout all this trekking, with two donkeys to one saddle, they never had a sore back.

On our arrival at Mani-Mani we found the Swahili village almost deserted. Everyone was out on a raid. They had reckoned that no one in their senses would return to the wilderness so soon as I had. They could not conceive how I had spent the proceeds of all that ivory in so short a time. I learnt that they were out against the Dabossans in whose country I meant to hunt. I therefore laid out my route so as to intercept the returning raiders.

Passing through Bukora we were greeted as old friends, a very different reception from our first. Pyjalé immediately joined up, and after taking a few good bull elephants from the Bukora-Kumamma neutral zone we trekked leisurely and heavily laden northwards.

At the last village of Bukora we met commotion and wailing. The occasion was the murder of three young Bukora girls of marriageable age at the hands of some roving band of Jiwé bloods. These affairs were of quite common occurrence, and the natives could never understand the disgust and abhorrence they drew from me. I was eventually able to stop the killing of females, at least while I was in the country.

Pitching camp late one night in the fighting zone between Bukora and Jiwé, lions were sighted leaving the rocky hills for the game-covered plains. Although almost dark I succeeded in killing two within a short distance of camp. I returned and was seated by the camp-fire when I heard alarming shouts from the direction of the dead lions. In this kind of life something is constantly turning up, and one soon learns to be always ready. The occurrences are so simple as to require but simple remedies. Everything seems to demand the presence of a rifle and just an ordinary sense of humour to transform an imminent tragedy into African comedy. Seizing my ·275 I rushed through the darkness towards the shouts, and what I found was that one lion had been skinned and the other half flayed when it had suddenly come to life again. The boys said that as they were removing its skin it suddenly and without warning stood up, opened its mouth and rushed at them. But what I found was a half-skinned lion with its head alive but the rest of it dead or paralysed. It could open its mouth and growl ferociously. Its springing at them must have been supplied by the boys' imaginations or to excuse their headlong flight. Some nerve must have suffered damage in the lion's neck, leaving the body paralysed but the head active. One of the boys had been seated on it when it growled, and his account of the affair in camp raised bursts of deep-chested Nyamwezi laughter.

These camps in the wonderful African nights of the dry season linger in my memory as the most enjoyable I have ever experienced. Other nights have been more exciting and more exhilarating, but also more harmful in their after-effects. Poker or flying by night, sitting up for elephant or lion, provide quicker pulse-beats between periods of intense boredom, but for level quiet enjoyment give me the camp-chair by the camp-fire with a crowd of happy and contented natives about and the prospect of good hunting in front and the evidence of good hunting by your side. Looking back on my safaris I can discern that they were quite exceptionally happy little collections of human beings. For one reason, health was simply splendid. Everyone was well and amply tented. All slept warm and dry. Mosquitoes were rare and stomachs full. Fun was of poor calibre, perhaps, but high animal spirits were there to make the most of it. The boys had their women—wives they called them. Tobacco could be traded from the natives or bought at cost price from the safari slop-chest.

Fighting among the men was always settled in the ring and with 4 oz. gloves provided by me. When this was found too slow —and they sometimes pounded each other for an hour on end, rounds being washed out—sticks were provided and the thing brought to a head more rapidly with the letting of a little blood. When the women bickered too persistently a ring would be formed, permission got and the two naggers dragged in. Each would then hitch up short her cloth about her ample hips and, after being provided with a hippo-hide whip, at it they would go with fire almost equal to that of the men. But with this difference. Where the men used their heads and tried to prevent the other from injuring them, the women waited motionless and guardless for each other's strokes. It was the most extraordinary form of fighting ever seen. A. would catch B. a stinging swinger on the back and stand waiting for B. to give her a frightful cut across the shoulders. And so on it would go—szwip! szwop!—for about ten minutes, when B. would suddenly cast her whip on the ground and flee, A. in hot pursuit, while shouts of laughter greeted the decision, especially strong when either combatant lost her last shred of cloth. I must say the women never bore malice and were always great friends afterwards. Even during the fighting they never showed vice, for they could as easily as not have cut the eye out of their unguarded opponent. Yet I never saw anything approaching an injury inflicted in these affairs.

Then in the evenings there was football. When I first introduced this game I tried to teach them rugger. They were born rugger players. Fast, bare-footed, hard, muscular and slippery, they cared not at all for the ant-heaps, boulders, or thorn bushes which littered their day's playground. After carrying a hundred-weight all day, pitching camp, building thorn bomas for the animals and bringing in firewood for the night, they would go to rugger until dark. So bad were some of the injuries sustained, owing to the bad terrain, that a new game had to be evolved more suited to the ground. After various trials a game was settled upon which seemed to suit. It was simply a kind of massed rush in which any number could engage. Goals were marked out at distances one from the other to suit the ground. Then the ball was placed at half-way and the two opposing sides drawn up in line about 15 yds. from it. At a signal both sides charged full tilt at each other, meeting about where the ball was. Then the object was to get the ball by hook or by crook to the goal. No off-side, no boundaries, no penalties, no referee and no half-time. Darkness terminated the game. So hard was the ground and so incessant the wear on the ball that it was seldom one lasted a month. How they could kick it without breaking their toes always puzzled me.

Our reputation had preceded us, and we were welcomed by the Jiwé people. So much so that they wished for blood-brotherhood, but I evaded it. We hunted happily in their country for some time and learnt of an attack on their country by a Nile tribe with numerous guns of muzzle-loading type. The Jiwé with spears alone had not only repulsed the attackers but had massacred most of them. Inadequate supplies of munitions had been their downfall. The firearms which had been picked up by the Jiwé had since been traded off to Swahilis.

While chasing elephant in the Jiwé country one day we happened to start some ostrich running. They took the same line as the fleeing elephant and soon overhauled them. When close up the cock bird suddenly began the fantastic dashes here and there usually seen in the breeding season. One of his speed efforts took him close past a lumbering bull elephant on the outside of the little herd. These elephants had already been severely chased and several of their number had been killed. When, therefore, the black form of the ostrich raced up from behind him the poor old elephant nearly fell over with fright. His trunk shot out and his ears looked like umbrellas turned inside out by a sudden gust. But recovering almost instantly, he settled back to his steady fast retreat.

Our next country northwards was Dodose, where I proposed to establish the base camp. On entering it we found it high-lying country among steep little granite hills. We were well received and soon became friendly. Some wonderful elephant country was reached from Dodose, and it was here that I got my heaviest ivory. Buffalo were also very numerous. It was beautiful hunting country, as elephant could frequently be found, with glasses, from one of the numerous hills.

It was now the dry season; there was, for that reason, only one route to or from Dabossa, where the Swahili raid was on. I therefore put a look-out post on this route to bring me news of anyone coming south on this trail. This post consisted of four of my best Wanyamweze boys with two natives. As soon as any sign of the returning raiders was seen the boys were to send a native with the news while they remained to try to keep any Swahilis until my arrival. I had expected the raiders to have a fore-guard of some sort and that I would have time to arrive on the scene between its arrival and the coming of the main body. Instead of this, up marched the whole body of raiders, cattle and captives, all in charge of my four stalwarts. What they had told the Swahilis lay in store for them I never learnt, but it was evidently something dreadful, judging by the state of panic they were in. I counted their guns and took their captives—all women—and cattle from them, warned them that next time they would land up in prison or be shot, and sent them packing.

After a considerable hunt in and around Dodose, it was now time, the first rains being imminent, to be moving northwards towards Dabossa. In entering new country for elephant it is always best to get there when the first rains are on, as the animals then desert their dry-season thick haunts for the open country.

Before approaching the inhabited part of Dabossa I knew that it would be necessary somehow to get into communication with the natives. They had just recently been raided and would be very nervous and likely to attack any strangers approaching their country. The Dabossan cattle recently taken from the raiders were therefore placed in the charge of some of the Dodose notables, while I and a good little safari headed northwards, taking with us all the captive women.

When still about forty miles from Dabossa it became evident from signs that Dabossans were about. We therefore camped by water and built a strong thorn boma. Everyone was warned not to leave the boma at night, but one of my personal boys—a brainless Kavirondo—thinking perhaps that orders were not meant for him, broke camp and was promptly speared. His cries effectually roused the camp, but the extent of his hurt bore little resemblance to the volume of his noise. He had a nice little spear thrust in a tender spot.

The boy's misfortune was promptly turned to account, for, after stilling his cries, we got the Dabossan captives to shout into the night all our news. Our reason for being there, our intentions, how we had their cattle ready to return to their owners—so far had the narrative got when first one voice from the dark and then others began asking for news of such and such a cow or heifer, so-and-so's bull or bullock. Later women or girl captives were asked after. Eventually men appeared and were persuaded to come to camp. Relations became friendly almost at once. At daybreak it was arranged for some of the natives to go at once to Dabossa and spread the news, while others accompanied some of my boys back to Dodose in order to identify their cattle. This was thought necessary as we did not know the cattle from any others, and also because it was almost certain that the Dodose notables would try to palm off their duds in place of the good Dabossan animals. Meanwhile I remained hunting the surrounding country.

In a few days there arrived a runner from Dodose with the news that my Dodose notables had held a meeting and, courage brewed by numbers and beer, had flatly refused to give up the Dabossan cattle left in their charge. Not knowing my native gentlemen quite as well as I ought to have, and that courage so rapidly got was as rapidly lost, I was on the point of rushing back to Dodose when another runner arrived saying that all was well and that notable after notable had singly and surreptitiously returned the full tally of cattle left with him.   I was relieved to hear this, as these constant native palavers were taking up a great deal of my hunting time.

The cattle soon arrived, drank up our small pool of water, and we pushed off all together for Dabossa.   The captive women were now, of course, quite free to go or stay and, without exception, they remained with us in idleness until removed by their men folk on our arrival in Dabossa.   Had I allowed it, most of them would have remained as " wives " to my men rather than go back to the heavy work of tilling in their home gardens.

We had a huge reception in Dabossa.   There must have been close on 5,000 spears assembled in the huge open space where we camped.   Pow-wows were the order of one long weary day when the cattle were handed over and the captives returned to their relations.   Peace for us at any rate was assured, but when I told the Dabossans that no one would attack them and that they ought to trade peacefully, they swore they would massacre every Swahili who might venture near their country.   After I had explained my wish to hunt elephant, an old woman got up and made a long speech to the effect that they owed everything to me and that they ought to give me a pair of tusks.   This they did, not particularly large ones.   But what was better than tusks was guides to the Murua Akipi (Mountain of Water) country, said to abound in elephant.

This Murua Akipi was the aim of my journey.   I had heard of it from native sources.   It was a wonderful country where anything might happen.   Huge elephant lived there.   Bad Abyssinians came there.   Elephant cemeteries were to be found there.   Water which killed whoever drank it was there and which looked so cold and clear.   No white man had ever seen it, although every traveller was supposed to be trying to reach it for the mysterious " thahabu " (gold) it contained.   In fact, if one asked for anything under the sun anywhere within a radius of one hundred miles he would be referred to that mysterious blue peak, Murua Akipi.

We trailed along through monotonous cultivated country for several days. Then coming to the end of Dabossa we entered on an exceptionally large deserted zone. Here hardly anyone ventured, as Habashi (Abyssinian) prowlers might be met. For several days the large open cotton-soil plains, with bands of thorn bush, were covered with great numbers of ostrich and topi haartebeeste. Abyssinians had recently raided the outskirts of Dabossa and all the boys were rather nervous, having heard dreadful tales of the Habashi.

We were not long in coming on signs of Habashi methods. Away over the plains some small black objects were seen. Zeiss showed them to be people, apparently women, seated on the ground. At closer range there were seven of them, all young women. Closer still, they appeared to be bound in a sitting posture, and all were in a very bad state. For one thing, their tongues all protruded and were black and fly covered. This was thirst. Their arms were passed inside the knee and were lashed securely to the outside of the ankle, and so used they were abandoned in this shameless fashion to rescue on the one hand or death from thirst on the other.

Having water with us we soon released them and gradually forced sufficient moisture between tongue and teeth. Contrasted with those dreadful tongues how perfectly beautiful primitive man's teeth appeared. Small, regular and widely set apart from each other, nothing seems to tarnish their whiteness.

These hardy creatures soon recovered sufficiently to stand up, and we packed each on a donkey to our next camp, where sufficient water for all was got. The next day we sent them off to their homes, feeling pretty certain there could be no Abyssinians between us and Dabossa, as water was still scarce.

We now sighted Murua Akipi as a minute tooth of pale blue just cutting the horizon. I thought we would reach it in two days, but it required four days of long marching to reach a small kopje a few miles from its base. That tiny tooth grew larger and larger each day until it looked an enormous size. I daresay it is not more than 2,000 or 3,000 ft., but being surrounded by huge plains it shows to great advantage.

One day while crossing the plains we had a smart shower which turned the black powdery soil into very tenacious mud. Walking became a trial for anything but naked feet, and I asked Pyjalé if the conditions were right for running down antelope. He assured me they were, and I urged him and the Dabossans to try it when opportunity arose. This was not long, for as we came out of a thorn belt we surprised a herd of eland and topi. Off went Pyjalé and the Dabossans, taking off their spear-guards as they ran. Off went the antelope, too, and for some time Pyjalé and Co. lost ground. Through my glasses I could see that the eland threw up much more mud than the topi and the topi much more than the natives. These latter hardly ever lifted a clod, whereas the galloping eland hove great masses into the air at every lurch. Consummate runners as all the natives were, Pyjalé was easily best. He could probably have closed with his beast sooner than he did but for his running it in a circle for my benefit. The heavy and fat eland were soon blown, and Pyjalé presently ranged alongside and with a neat and lightning dart of his spear thrust it to the heart. The movement was barely perceptible through the glass.

While on the subject of native runners I would like to tell what took place at Kampala, the capital of Uganda, in the year when Dorando won the marathon in England. Everyone was marathon mad, and the fever spread to Uganda. A marathon for native runners was organised as part of the attractions of the Show. Native chiefs were warned to seek out and train any likely talent they might have. The training consisted of feeding the runners largely on beef.

The course was from Enteble to Kampala show ground with one complete circuit of the ground. The course was carefully marked and two whites on bicycles were told off to ride with the runners. The distance, I believe, was almost exactly the same as the English course. About thirty runners started in the hottest part of the day, experienced heavy rain en route, which turned the road to mud and washed out the bicycles, and thirty runners arrived *together* at the show ground, tore round the ground singing and leaping in the air, fresh as paint, completed the course still all together, and went on circling the ground, thinking they were giving their lady friends a treat I suppose. They had to be stopped eventually, but the most astonishing thing was that their time for the course was almost exactly Dorando's time, if I remember rightly. They thought it was better fun to come in all together than by ones and twos.

Camp was pitched at the foot of the kopje, sufficient rain water being found in the elephant baths for all our requirements. The next morning I climbed the little hill in pouring rain. From its top I had a good view of the Murua to the south, while to the north a river was visible flowing northwards. On its banks were large verdant green flats which might have been as smooth as tennis lawns but for the fact that they were thickly speckled with black dots which the glasses and then the telescope showed to be the backs and heads of scores of bull elephant. The grass consequently was young swamp grass and about six or seven feet high. The big tripod telescope showed some wonderful ivory, and I have never seen before or since so many *old* bull elephant in one place. Bunches of young herd bulls were comparatively common, but here were numbers of aged bulls.

Knowing how all naked men hate rain, I left Pyjalé in camp and took instead a well-clad boy whose feet had worn off earlier in the journey, and who had since been recuperating at the base camp. Nothing takes condition off a naked African like heavy rain. Strong as their constitutions are they wilt when constantly wet once the natural oil of the skin is pierced.

Striking straight for the swamps through the thorny flats we came out of some very dense wait-a-bit almost under the trunk of a single old monster. I thought of trying a shot up through the palate for the brain, but wisely refrained and withdrew quickly a few paces while the old bull stared straight at us, still unsuspicious, and affording an easy frontal shot.

Passing on, we were presently on the edge of the green swamp. And now how different the smooth-looking lawn appeared; huge broad-leaved grass, still young, but seven or eight feet high in places. While all the dry country was still parched after the long dry season, here on this rich flood-land the grass had two or three months' start. Hence the numbers of elephant. But why only bulls? That is known to them only. I had a grand day among them in spite of the grass. Soaked to the skin, the temperature just suited the white man, and I returned washed out but happy to a comfortable tent, hot bath, dry towels and pyjamas, food ready and good enough for keen appetite and the best of service. Off with wet and mud-covered things, dump them on the ground-sheet; good boys are there ready to pick them up, wash them and dry them by the huge camp-fire. Fresh clothes every day—what real solid comfort one has in the bush! No laundry bills to face and no clothes to be careful of. Creases in the trousers not required below the knee, and the harder the usage the softer the wear. Having tasted Heaven already I think I must be booked for the other place. Ten good tails was the count for the day.

Mounting Look-out Hill next morning, no elephant was visible, so off went the cutting-out gang with their axes, etc., and my yesterday's companion as guide to the slain. In the evening they returned with some magnificent ivory, but having found only nine carcases. Having the tails of ten, I thought they had failed to find the tenth, and I turned in, meaning to show them it on the morrow. I remembered now on looking at the ivory that the missing animal had exceptionally long tusks. I had measured them with my fore-arm, and three and a half lengths had they protruded from the lip. Resolved to find him, we searched the whole area of that swamp, but nowhere could he be found. At last I came to the spot from which I had fired, as I supposed, the fatal shot. After a little search I found the empty ·275 case. There a few yards away should have been the elephant. Here was where he lay on his side; grass flattened, mark of under tusk in mud, all complete. But no elephant could be found. It was a case of stun and nothing else. And there on those plains there probably wanders to this day an elephant distinguished from other tailless elephants by having had his tail painlessly amputated by human hand and Sheffield cutlery while under the influence of a unique anæsthetic. Meanwhile I had lost two grand tusks. One of the other bulls had a single tooth only, but almost made up for this fraudulent shortage by weighing in 134 lb. for his single tooth. The weight for the nine bulls was 1,463 lb., all first-rate stuff, and the value then in London somewhere about £877.

After some fairly successful hunting in the neighbourhood it was time to move on to the wonderful mountain. Its wonder had somewhat eased off by our close contact. Indeed, it now appeared as just an ordinary-looking African hill, extremely sterile and forbidding-looking. Although from a distance it had appeared as an isolated peak, on closer acquaintance there were seen to be not a few foot-hills of insignificant height. It was on the spur of one of these that we met with Abyssinians. As we headed across the plains men were seen scuttling up the rocks, and my glasses showed mules tethered some way up. We were therefore about to encounter our first Abyssinians. Everyone was in a twitter. Habashi have a truly awful reputation for nameless atrocities in those parts, and had it lain with them my safari would have chosen instant flight rather than come within rifle-shot of those mounted terrors. For my part, I felt tolerably all right, as the glasses showed no sign of the enemy being in any force. And then I thought that if I were in their place and saw a safari of our size marching resolutely towards me I should feel pretty anxious. This thought comforted me to such an extent that I did a foolish thing.

I was at that time trying to get a really good pair of oryx horns, and when almost under the noses of the Abyssinians lying in the rocks up got a good oryx and I let drive. Too late, the thought that the enemy might think I was firing at them flashed through my mind. I rushed up to the fallen buck and seemed busy with it. As a matter of fact, we subsequently found that the great, fierce, bold Abyssinians were in a much greater funk than we were. We shouted in Arabic that we were friends, and invited them to come down. We tried everything without success, and at last camped peacefully beneath them. As evening was drawing on and they had not yet come I strolled up to the mules without arms in case they might be scared. Then I sat down and smoked, hoping they would join me. But no, all I could see of them was their heads among the rocks. I went slowly towards them, and when I was quite close I found the poor devils were literally shivering. Good Heavens! I thought, what devilment have you been up to, to be in such a state? It was only by sitting down with them in their funk holes and chewing coffee berries which they offered that they could be persuaded to come forth. But at last they came to camp and settled down. It was impossible to talk with them. They knew no Arabic, and we knew no Abyssinian. However, we made out that they were ten days' ride from their base and were out for elephant. Slaves, in other words, I suspect. They made me a present of a goodish young mule with saddle and bridle complete and a French Daudeter rifle, while I gave them in return a fine tusk. We parted, mutually relieved to see the last of each other.

At the end of a short march across lava-dust plains we reached the wonderful mountain Murua Akipi. Skirting the base of it, we found a fine, well-worn elephant road, which we followed for some miles, until a branch led us up a gully to a little level plain surrounded by rocky lava-strewn hill-slopes of a most forbidding description. For a few yards in the centre of the plain there was some very short and verdant green grass dotted here and there by the white bleached skulls of elephant while half-buried leg bones showed their huge round knuckle ends. In the centre of this green oasis were three pools of intensely clear green water. All round the edges of the grass there were glistening lines of white powder, evidently high-water marks. I tasted the water; it was certainly very bitter.

Here was what native information called an elephant cemetery, and at first sight I thought it was. But on looking round and thinking it over a bit I was first struck by the fact that there were no recent bones or skulls. Again, all the skulls seemed to have undergone about the same amount of weathering. I talked it over with Pyjalé, and he told me that he had heard from the old men who had had it from others that once there came a dreadful drought upon the land; that so scarce had water become that springs of the nature in question were the only ones left running, and that they then became so strong that animals and men drinking of their waters immediately died. Even now as we drank it in a normal season the water was very bitter, although it appeared to have no after-effect beyond acting as a slight aperient. Natron is, I believe, the impregnation. So much for the elephant cemeteries.

Still skirting the base of Murua Akipi on well-worn elephant paths, we next day sighted zebra high up on the mountain side. Halting the safari I went to investigate and found a pool of fresh water, sufficiently large for several days. Here we camped, and from this spot I did the mountain. From its top away to the north-east could be seen a distant line of hills which I took to be Abyssinia. To the N.W. I could trace the course of the river which had afforded such good results in elephant. It meandered away through huge open plains until lost in the distance. I imagine it must flow into the Akobo or Pibor. At the time of which I write the maps were a blank as regards this region.

With my eyes well skinned for gold I washed the gravel in the pot-holes of the stream beds but without result. Soon tiring of this prospecting I began to search the surrounding country for

game. With clear atmosphere and good glasses all kinds of game
were seen. The dry lava-dust plains were covered with herds of
oryx, ostrich, giraffe and gazelle. In the thorn belts elephant were
seen. To find game I used prismatic binoculars, and to examine
the animals more closely I had a large telescope on a tripod. With
this I could almost weigh the tusks of elephant seven or eight miles
distant. It was most fascinating to watch the animals through
this glass. Sometimes rhino would be seen love-making. The
inclination was to spend too much time at the eye-piece. But
what dances that glass led me. I would watch two or three heavy
old bull elephant feeding slowly about. It looked absurdly easy
to go down to the plain and walk straight to them. But this I knew
was not so, and I would try to memorise the country which lay
between me and the animals. But however I tried it was always
most difficult to find them once the flat was reached. Everything
altered and looked different.

My hunting round Murua Akipi was so successful that I found
my safari already too heavily laden to attempt the following of the
north-flowing river. Only in these two particulars—the presence
of large elephant and Abyssinians—had the wondermongers been
right about Murua Akipi. Gold was not found. The deadly
waters were merely natron springs. The elephant cemeteries had
been cemeteries during one exceptionally dry season only, or so it
seemed.

For a hunter well equipped with food stuffs a hunt of three
months' duration in the country surrounding Murua Akipi would
have shown astonishing results. As it was we carried with us flour
traded on Mt. Elgon, some 600 miles south of us. Of course
everyone was on half rations, that is every boy received a condensed
milk tin half filled with banana flour for the one day with the addition of as much elephant meat and fat or buck meat as he cared to
take. In addition to this everyone got salt. The condition of all
was magnificent. My food was arranged for in the following
manner. There were four milk cows constantly in milk. As they

went dry they were exchanged for others from the native herds. Two of these cows, with their calves, accompanied me wherever I went; while two rested at the base camp in Dodose. Hence I always had milk, the staple of all the native tribes. In time I came to drink it as they did, that is sour. Mixed with raw blood as they took it, I could never master, although it then becomes a perfect food I am convinced. Fresh milk as we drink it at home is regarded by all pastoral tribes in the light of a slow but sure poison. They all declare that the drinking of milk in its fresh state leads to anæmia and loss of power. Under no conditions will they drink it fresh, but will always stand it in a calabash where it soon sours.

My two cows were milked night and morning. The evening milking was put to stand in a calabash and was sour by morning. The calabash was carried by a boy and I drank it about 9 a.m. after marching from about 6 a.m. This I found did me well throughout the day without anything else, and no matter how hard the travelling. It seemed a perfect food. One did not get thirsty as after a meat meal, neither did one become soon hungry as after a farinaceous meal. Meanwhile that morning's milk was carried in a calabash all day and was " ripe " for the evening's meal. Then round the camp fire I would frizzle dry buck-meat in the embers.

A boy's feeding arrangements were as follows : He would wake up about 2 a.m., having slept since about 8 p.m. On his camp fire he would warm up a chunk of smoked elephant or buck meat. This he would not touch until the first halt in the day's march, generally about 9 a.m. He would then have this first meal, consisting entirely of smoked beef. After that he would perform his hard day's work. In the evening at sun-down his flour, if on half rations, would be made into thin gruel with fat added and a pinch of wild tamarind to "mustard" it. When on full rations thick porridge stiffened *off* the fire with raw flour would be made, after that more smoked meat. Here again absolutely fresh meat was never eaten, always the smoked or dried meat.

As regards the thirst-resisting qualities of the grain and meat diet as opposed to the milk and meat diet there was no comparison. Pyjalé, who shared my milk, once went three days without either food or drink, whereas a grain-eating boy who became lost was rescued just in time after only thirty-six hours without water.

After consulting the donkey-headman it was decided that we had almost as much ivory as we could carry. Many of the tusks were too long for donkeys and should have been taken by porters. It was decided to return to our base through untouched country. The news was received with shouts of joy. It is wonderful how one comes to regard the base camp as home. Whereas, on our way up, the camps had been rather gloomy—disasters having been prophesied for this expedition—now all was joy. The safari chronicler became once more his joyous self and his impromptu verse became longer and longer each night. The chronicler's job is to render into readily chanted metre all the important doings of the safari and its members. It is a kind of diary and although not written down is almost as permanent, when committed to the tenacious memories of natives. Each night, in the hour between supper and bedtime, the chronicler gets up and blows a vibrating blast on his waterbuck horn. This is the signal for silence. All is still. Then begins the chant of the safari's doings, verse by verse, with chorus between. It is extraordinarily interesting but very difficult to understand. The arts of allusion and suggestion are used most cleverly. In fact, the whole thing is wonderful. Verse by verse the history rolls out on the night, no one forgetting a single word. When the well-known part is finished, bringing the narrative complete up to and including yesterday, there is a pause of expectation—the new verse is about to be launched. Out it comes without hesitation or fault, all to-day's events compressed into four lines of clever metric *précis*. If humorous its completion is greeted with a terrific outburst of laughter and then it is sung by the whole lot in chorus, followed by a flare-up of indescribable noises; drums, pipes, horns and human voices. And then to bed, while those keen-eyed camp askaris mount guard; although they cannot hit a mountain by daylight they fire *and kill* by night with a regularity that always leaves me dumb with astonishment. Remember they are using ·450 bore bullets in ·577 bore barrels, and explain it who can. They call it "medicine."

We traversed some queer country on our return to Dodose. All kinds were met with. We went thirty days on end without seeing an elephant, and in the succeeding four days I killed forty-four bulls. A lioness came within a foot of catching a boy and was shot. The dried skins of elephant were found occupying much the same position as when filled with flesh. Now they contained nothing but the loose bones, all the meat having been eaten away by maggots and ants, which had entered through nature's ports. Why the skin had not rotted as in other parts I could but ascribe to the dryness of the atmosphere. Finally, we staggered home, heavily laden with ivory, to our base camp.

That safari was one of my most successful. We "shuka'd," or went down country, with over 14,000 lbs. of ivory—all excellent stuff.

VII

THROUGH THE SUDD OF THE GELO RIVER

AT the time of which I write, about 1908, the wild countries lying around the western and south-western base of the Abyssinian plateau seemed to us to present the most favourable field of operations. And as the boundaries had not yet been delimited between Abyssinia and the Sudan on the one hand and Abyssinia and Uganda on the other, we felt that there would be more scope for our activities in that region than elsewhere. The object was elephant hunting.

In order to reach this country we were obliged to cross Abyssinia. We took steamer to Djibuti on the Red Sea, ascending thence by railway to the then railhead, Dirré Doua, and then by horse, camel and mule to Addis Abeba, the capital. Here, the only trouble we had was from our own legation. Our representative regarded every English traveller in the light of being a potential source of trouble to him personally, and was at little pains to conceal his thoughts. Luckily, we had been recommended financially to the bank, and this fact smoothed our path. Apparently, in these matters the main question is whether one is the possessor of a few hundred pounds or not. If so, zeal in helping the traveller on is forthcoming; but if not, every obstacle is put in the way of his ever making any progress. In one of our colonies I was once asked bluntly by the Government representative if I had any money. Of course, the poor man was merely trying to do his duty; but before I could think of this I had replied, " Precious little." Throughout my stay in his province he regarded me with the gravest suspicion.

Along the route from Addis Abeba to Goré in the west we were much pestered for presents by the Abyssinian military governors.

78

We had been warned about this and were supplied with some automatic pistols.   They invariably turned these down and tried to get our rifles, but as invariably accepted the pistols.   These gentry have to be reckoned with, as it is within their power to hold up the traveller by simply declaring the road to be dangerous.

At Goré we came under the rule of the famous chief Ras Tasama. He reigned over the whole of the western part of Abyssinia, tolerating no interference from the Emperor, but paying to him a considerable tribute.   This tribute was mainly composed of slaves, gold dust and ivory.   The dust was gathered annually from the river beds, after the rains, and by the subject races.   We were informed that Goré's quota amounted to 4,000 oz.   Ivory was obtained from the negro tribes living in the lowlands below the Abyssinian plateau. One chief with whom we came in contact was required to provide 300 tusks annually, and apparently could do so easily.   It will give an idea of the immense numbers of elephant in the country when I mention that this chief had under him quite a modest little tribe, occupying a country which could be traversed in four days of easy marching.

Slaves were raided from tribes which could not or would not provide ivory.   We gathered that these raids were extremely brutal affairs, for which the Abyssinian habits of eating raw meat and drinking rawer alcohol seemed peculiarly to fit them, and that just before our arrival at Goré a raid had resulted in the capture of 10,000 men, women and children.   This figure is probably an exaggeration, but it was evident from the accounts of witnesses whom we questioned that the numbers must have been very considerable. They said that the mules, with children lashed on them like faggots, required half the day to pass through the town.   The only sign of slaving that we ourselves saw was when we met a body of mounted Abyssinians guarding some wild-looking natives from some distant land.   Even if their patient phlegm and air of despair had not drawn our attention to them, the fact that they were completely nude, very black, and wore ornaments such as necklaces made up of countless little round discs of ostrich eggshell, otherwise unseen in Abyssinia, would have done so.   We were spared the sight of children.

From information gathered, it now became necessary to obtain permission from Ras Tasama to proceed off the beaten track for the purpose of hunting elephant.   So far we had followed the well beaten Addis-Gambela-Khartoum track.   We stated our wishes at the first interview with the Ras.   He was an imposing-looking old man, short of stature, but with the expression of power, authority and dignity so often found in outstanding Africans.   Accompanied by our one-eared interpreter, who had lost the other as a punishment for having sided with the Italians in the war, we were received in the hall of his house, a two-storeyed building of oval shape and a fine specimen of Abyssinian architecture.   The usual compliments passed between us and the customary present was duly presented by us.   It took the form, on this occasion, of a case of liqueur brandy and a little banker's bag containing fifty golden sovereigns. As is usual in Africa, the gifts were received without demonstration. We then proceeded to state our business, through our interpreter. We were elephant hunters and wished to have the Ras's permission to hunt and his advice on where to go.   Drinks were served.   Our choice was old *tedg* (honey-mead), the national drink.   It was clear and sparkling, very good and rather like champagne.   The Ras told us it was nine years old.   He himself preferred *araki*, which is almost pure alcohol flavoured with aniseed.   He then remarked that he knew of a country where there were many elephant.   This remark we thought distinctly promising, but he made no further reference to the subject of so much importance to us.   The visit ended.

On our return to camp we asked our interpreter what we should do now.   He said we would get what we wanted, but that we should give the Ras another present.   We looked about and finally decided to give him one of our sporting rifles.   Next day, after arranging to call on him, we duly presented this beautiful weapon together with a lot of cartridges.   More hope was doled out to us, without anything definite happening.   And so on it went for three weeks. By that time the Ras had become possessed of eight mules, fifteen camels (he asked for these), several firearms and sundry cases of liquor, besides the presents first mentioned.   We were then at the end of our resources and in desperation.   This the Ras probably knew as well as we did, for at long last the desired permission was given.   But only verbally and without witnesses.   Once he had given his word, however, the thing was thoroughly well done.   A guide was provided to take us to the hunting grounds.   This man not only guided us, but as long as we remained in country owing allegiance to the Ras we were provided with everything the country afforded.

After descending the steep edge of the Abyssinian Plateau we arrived at the rolling plains, several thousands of feet lower and very much hotter than Goré.   Mosquitoes were to be reckoned with once more.   The natives were now very black, naked, Nilotic and pagan, but paid tribute to Ras Tasama in ivory.

The guide furnished us by Ras Tasama took us to the chief of these people.   He was a great swell and wore an Abyssinian robe. While at his village he fêted us and our Abyssinians, and in the night came secretly to ask if we wished to buy ivory.   We replied guardedly that much depended on the price asked.   He then sent for a tusk and we were overjoyed to see that the ivory of the country was large and soft.   We asked if that was all he had.   He said he had more.   Could we see it?   Yes, and he led us to a stockade where he had a considerable amount of tusks hidden in a hole and covered with mats.   One was very large—about 150 lb., I would say. We then asked him what he wanted for his ivory. " Guineea," he said.   It took us some time before it dawned on us.   He wanted guineas, as English or Egyptian sovereigns are called.   We were astonished, and wondered how he was acquainted with them.   It appeared that at Gambela there was a Greek trader who apparently bought ivory and it was there that our friend had dealt in sovereigns. But of their true value he was ignorant, evidently confusing them

with some smaller coin as he asked for an impossible number for a
tusk.   We knew that this chief was in high favour with Ras Tasama
and that he paid tribute of 300 tusks annually.   This fact, combined
with the sight before our eyes, seemed to denote enormous numbers
of elephant somewhere, and yet we had seen no tracks so far.   We
asked where all this ivory came from.   The chief smiled in a superior
way, telling us to wait and he would show us so many elephant that
we would be afraid to look upon them, let alone hunt them.

He was right about their numbers, for a few days after leaving
his village we came upon the trail of a roaming herd.   The well-
beaten part of this trail was literally several hundreds of yards wide.
I am afraid to estimate how many animals must have been in that
herd.

Although it was several days old I wanted to follow it.   I took it
to be a migration of sorts.   But the natives said no, there was no
need to.   There were plenty more.   And, sure enough, they were
right.   We arrived at a small village on the banks of the Gelo.

Looking up our map we found that the Gelo River from Lake
Tata down-stream was marked as unknown.   Accordingly, we
made enquiries among the natives about the country down-stream,
and were told that there were no natives for many days, that the
whole country was under water at this season and that no one
would go.

This was good enough for us.   We opened negotiations with the
chiefs for some dug-out canoes, which we obtained for various sun-
dries.   They were poor carriers and very crank, so I lashed them
together in rafts of three.

It was now necessary to deal with our followers.   All the Abyssinians would have to return as they were daily becoming more fever-
stricken.   With them would go the mules.   The guide rightly considered he had done his job.   There remained four of my old Swahili
followers from British East Africa, who had been shipped, through
Thos. Cook and Son, from Mombassa to Djibuti, and four Yemen
Arabs we had picked up on our way through.   The Swahilis were

old hands, had been everywhere with me for about ten years, and cared not a rap where we went. The Arabs were new, but splendid fellows. They hated the thought of recrossing Abyssinia by themselves and were, therefore, obliged to go on with us.

On loading up the flotilla it was found impossible to carry all our stores. We made a huge bonfire of the surplus, and I well remember how well the ham and bacon burned. We regretted burning all these good things, but, as a matter of fact, we were better without them. Laying in a stock of native grain we pushed off into the current and swung down-stream.

It was the rainy season and the discomforts we suffered were sometimes acute. Almost immediately on quitting the chief's village we entered a region where hard ground rose only a few inches above water level. Great areas were entirely covered by water, only the tops of the 12-foot grass showing above it. Whenever we turned one of the many bends of the river, and these were hard banks, there would be a continuous line of splashes, which advanced with us as the crocodiles plunged in. The waters teemed with fish, especially the lung-fish, which continued rising night and day to breathe, as we supposed.

In this swamp country every night was a time of horror, and camping a perfect nightmare. Well before the sun was down the mosquitoes appeared in myriads. Luckily our boys had each been provided with a mosquito net. These nets I had procured with a watertight canvas roof so that they also acted as small tents. They could be slung between sticks or paddles stuck in the ground. Without these nets no man could long survive the quite serious loss of blood and sleep; for, to add to our troubles, firewood was non-existent. In the hot, sweltering nights, when it was not raining, the moon would appear almost obliterated by the clouds of mosquitoes hanging to the net, while the massed hum seemed to be continuous. And yet there was no fever among us, presumably because of the lack of infection sources. Several times no dry spot could be found and we stuck it out as best we could on the canoes.

Of game we saw nothing except elephant.   No buck or buffalo nor even hippo in that desolate region.   How numerous elephant were I cannot say, as we never hunted them unless we actually saw them from the canoes.   Low on the water as we were and with high grass everywhere, it was necessary for the animals to be within a few yards of the bank in order to come within our view.   Hunting thus we killed some 30 bulls as we drifted along.   Allowing that we killed half we saw, that would mean that 60 bull elephant crossed our narrow path at the moment we were there or thereabouts.   If the region were only a few miles deep on either bank and were frequented on a similar scale, it would indicate an enormous number of elephant.   We took little heed of cows, but of these quite a hundred came within our view.

All our boys being Mohammedans, we two whites were the only eaters of elephant meat.   Luckily for the others, fish were easily caught.

At one place where we killed elephant we found a raised piece of ground perhaps three or four feet above the water.   It even had three trees on it.   We were simply delighted to reach shore again, and as we had killed six good bulls that day the camp was merry— at any rate, the white portion of it.   As we were obliged to wait here three or four days for the elephant to rot before drawing the tusks, we pitched our tents and made everything comfortable.   In the night a terrific rain storm blew up, and when it was at its height red ants invaded us.   My companion was got first, and had to vacate his bed and tent.   I could hear him cursing between the thunder claps.   Presently he came into my tent, quite naked, as they had got into his pyjamas.   I told him to lay a trail of paraffin all round the tent, while I proceeded to tuck my net well in all round me.   As he was laying the trail the rising water came rushing in, bearing with it thousands of desperate ants.   They swarmed up everything they touched.   I lay, as I thought, secure, my companion fled, slapping and brushing his naked legs and cursing dreadfully.

For some time the enemy failed to penetrate my fine-mesh net, but when they did get me they all got me at once. Without two thoughts I was out in the pouring rain and throwing off my pyjamas. After brushing off the fiery hot devils I found they were mounting my legs just as fast. My companion yelled through the storm to get up on an up-turned bucket. I found one at last and mounted. And thus we rode it out.

There was bad "medicine" in that camp, for next day my companion got gassed when he drew a tusk, and was violently sick; and while carrying the tusk back to camp stepped on a huge fish, while wading through mud and water, which threw him headlong into it.

We were now obliged to cast gear in order to carry ivory. Spare axes, tools and camp gear went first, and finally provisions and tents. At last we could take nothing more aboard and float. We left fine ivory standing on the banks. We had formed the idea of returning, properly equipped, for this inland navigation, and headed down-stream with about two inches freeboard. Our sluggish Gelo bore us slowly into the sluggish Pibor which pushed us gently into the livelier Sobat. On our way down this river to the Nile we were so short of food and the usual wherewithal to buy it that we were obliged to part with one of our tusks for native grain, fowls, and a couple of sheep. We camped frequently by the villages of the Nuers, and were astonished to learn on our arrival at the Nile that we were then at war with this tribe.

I am inclined to think that we were rather lucky to have come through the sudd region of the Gelo so easily. At one place the open channel divided equally into two, and we debated which one we should follow. We tossed, and the paddle decided on the right-hand channel. We followed it, but never saw where the other channel rejoined.

After reaching the more open waters of the Sobat the lightest breeze raised sufficient lop on the water to come aboard with our dangerously low freeboard. As it was, we were caught about mid-stream once, and before we could reach the bank the whole flotilla settled down.   Luckily, we were only a few yards from shore and in about ten feet of water.   Our boys were magnificent, and got everything up while we plugged shots into the water to keep off crocs.   Had we foundered further out, the whole of our ivory and rifles, etc., would have been lost.

The hunting of elephant in this swamp region was of the severest description.   That is the reason of their congregating there in such numbers, I think.   The ground was too rotten for ponies or mules, even should they survive the myriads of flies and mosquitoes. The grass was mostly the 12-foot stuff with razor-like edges and countless, almost invisible spines, which stick into exposed limbs. Locomotion for humans was only possible when following elephant tracks.   When within even a few paces of the animals it was generally impossible to see them.   I used to mount on a boy's shoulder and fire from there, but the stance was so wobbly and the view so obstructed by grass tops as to make it most unsatisfactory. Having a large telescope mounted on a stout tripod I fitted a tiny board to fix on the tripod top, and found it most satisfactory; although the jump from my rifle, slight as it was, knocked me off once or twice.

On this safari the health of everyone was excellent, considering the hard work and poor food.   We whites were troubled somewhat with indigestion, caused I think by our native-grain flour having got wet, and fermented a bit.   There was practically no fever, and my tough old Swahilis came through without turning a hair.   The Arabs, however, lost condition.

VIII

THE LADO ENCLAVE

AT the time of which I write the Enclave de Lado comprised the country bordering the western bank of the Upper Nile from Lado on the north to Mahazi in the south. It was leased to Leopold, King of the Belgians, for the duration of his life and for six months after his death. This extension of the lease was popularly supposed to be for the purpose of enabling the occupiers to withdraw and remove their gear.

While the King was still alive and the Enclave occupied by the Congo authorities, I stepped ashore one day at Lado, the chief administrative post in the northern part. Luckily for me, the Chef de Zone was there, and I immediately announced my business, the hunting of elephant. The Chef was himself a great shikari, and told me he held the record for the (then) Congo Free State, with a bag of forty-seven, I think it was. He was most kind and keenly interested in my project, and promised to help in every way he could.

As regards permission to hunt, he told me that if I merely wished to shoot one or two elephants, he could easily arrange that on the spot, but that if I wanted to hunt elephant extensively, I should require a permit from the Governor, who lived at Boma, at the mouth of the Congo. The price of this permit was £20, and it was good for five months in one year. It was quite unlimited and, of course, was a gift to anyone who knew the game. The Belgians, however, seemed to think that the demanding of 500 frs. for a permit to hunt such dangerous animals was in the nature of pure extortion ; they regarded as mad anyone who paid such a sum for such a doubtful privilege.

I was, naturally, very eager to secure such a permit, especially when the Chef told me of the uncountable herds of elephants he had seen in the interior. By calculation it was found that the permit, if granted, would arrive at Lado in good time for the opening of the season, three months hence. I deposited twenty golden sovereigns with the Treasury, copied out a flowery supplication to the Governor for a permit, which my friend the Chef drafted for me, and there was nothing more to do but wait.

My visit to Lado was my first experience of Belgian domestic arrangements. The Chef de Zone lived entirely apart from the other officers, but with this exception they all messed together. The Chef himself was most exclusive; he gave me to understand, in fact, he regarded his subordinate whites as "scum." He gave me many cryptic warnings to have no dealings with them, all of which were rather lost on me then, as I had never hitherto come in contact with white men just like that. When, therefore, I was invited to dine at the mess I accepted, little knowing what I was in for.

The mess-room was a large room, or rather a large thatched roof standing on many pillars of sun-dried brick. In place of walls nothing more substantial than mosquito netting interposed itself between the diners and the gaze of the native multitude, comprising the station garrison, and so on. This system of architecture suits the climate admirably, its sole drawback being its publicity. For when the inmates of such a structure have the playful dinner habits of our forefathers, without their heads, and try to drink each other under the table, and when, moreover, the casualties are removed by native servants from that ignominious position one after the other, speechless, prostrate and puking, naturally the whole affair becomes a kind of "movie" show, with sounds added, for the native population. When, for instance, the Chef de Post, whose image is intimately connected in most of the spectators' minds with floggings, ambitiously tries to mount the table, fails and falls flat, the "thunders of applause" of our newspapers best describe the reception of his downfall by the audience.

At the dinner in question we started well. One member of the mess contributed five dozen of bottled beer. Another a case of whisky. A demi-john or two of the rough ration table wine rendered somewhat alcoholic by the vagaries of wine in the Tropics was also available ; but the effort of the evening was when a sporting Count produced a bottle of Curaçao. We sat down.

Directly in front of me, in the usual position, I found some plates, a knife, fork and spoon. But on three sides I was surrounded by eggs. There were, I think, three dozen of them. On looking round I observed that each diner was similarly provided. Then soup arrived, very strong, good and liberally flavoured with garlic. It was made from buffalo killed by the Post's native hunters. Meanwhile I noticed my neighbours handing out their eggs to the boys and giving instructions regarding them. I was at a loss. Hitherto I had regarded my eggs as being boiled and ready to eat, all the time mildly wondering how I was to eat so many. Then I caught the word omelette pass my neighbour's lips as he handed a dozen or two to the boy. I tumbled to it. They were raw and you simply handed them out as you fancied, to be turned into fried, poached, boiled eggs or omelettes. What a capital idea ! I set aside a dozen for an omelette, a half dozen to be fried, and a half dozen to be poached. I thought that if I got through that lot I should have enough.

The next dish appeared and was placed before the senior officer at the head of the table. It looked to me like a small mountain of mashed beetroot. Into its sugar-loaf apex the officer dug a large wooden salad spoon, turning in one rotary motion its perfect sugar-loaf shape into that of an extinct volcano. With deft and practised hand he then broke egg after egg, raw, into the yawning crater. His spare dozen or so were quickly swallowed up and more were supplied. As well as I could judge, the contents of the eggs were in no case examined. To anyone acquainted with the average African egg this means a lot.

On to the sulphur-splotched and quivering mass pepper and

salt were liberally poured; then vinegar and a vigorous stirring prepared it for presentation to the one bewildered and suffering guest. I took a moderate helping of the red crater slopes, avoiding the albuminous morass, wondering how you handled it anyhow and what would happen if you broke the containing walls. I watched the dish go the rounds with great interest, hoping someone would be too bold with the large spoon, prematurely burst the crater and be engulfed in the ensuing flood. But, alas! with marvellous dexterity man after man hoicked out a plateful of the nauseating stuff without accident. They were used to it.

Now I tried a taste of the minced beetroot lying before me. It wasn't beetroot at all. It was raw buffalo flesh. I did not like it awfully. Why, I do not know. I have always admired, theoretically, men who eat raw meat. When I saw the Abyssinians eating their meat raw I did not admire them particularly, and now when I saw the Belgians eating it raw I did not seem to admire them either. And yet when I read of Sandow and the crack boxers eating raw meat I admired them. Perhaps it is the sight of men eating raw meat which stops the admiration, or, perhaps, the men who can safely eat raw meat must be admirable to begin with. Anyhow, this lot revolted me, to the complete extinction of my usually robust appetite. It only recovered when cake was served up with syrup and you poured wine over it, an excellent sweet.

Drinking had meanwhile been going steadily on. I would say that by the time the cake came on each man had absorbed two litres of 18 per cent. wine. I was diligently pressed to drink, but managed to avoid more than my share. I excused myself by saying that I was not used to it, and had rather a light and unreliable head anyhow. As this was really a fact, I was rather astonished to notice that already some of the diners were beginning to show unmistakable signs of deep drinking. I subsequently discovered that while there was liquor in the station the drinking of it went on more or less night and day.

Towards the end of the meal some bottles of fine wine were produced and ran their course. After dinner beer was produced and diligently dealt with as a preliminary to the drinking of the case of whisky. This latter was regarded as serious drinking, requiring careful preparation. I have noticed the same curious attitude towards whisky in Frenchmen also. They affect to regard it as a frightfully potent and insidious drink. One will often see an absinthe-sodden toper take a ludicrously small tot of whisky, drowning it with a quart of water on the score of its great strength.

They began to taunt me with not drinking level. Stupid remarks were made about Englishmen and their inability to drink. I helped myself to a moderately large peg of whisky—which was good—and drank.

Now, they took this act to be a direct challenge. Here was a miserable Englishman taking far more whisky and far less water than they themselves were in the habit of taking. It was enough. The man to whom I passed the bottle had to go one better, taking a large peg; and so it went on progressing round the table until, about half-way, the bottle was finished. More were soon brought, uncorked and placed ready. When it came to a man opposite me I could see his hand tremble as with pale determination he poured out what he believed to be the strongest liquor in the world. With shouts of defiance the second bottle was drained, having passed up about four places. From noisy drinking the affair passed into a disorderly debauch. Diner after diner fell and was removed, until there remained seated but two men and myself. One was a Dane of fine physique, and the other was the Belgian Count. We looked at each other and smiled. We all thought we were strictly sober, but the Count, at any rate, was mistaken; for, when he rose to fetch another bottle of Curaçao from his boxes, he, too, joined the casualties. The Dane and I carried him to his bed, found his keys in his trouser pocket, unlocked his boxes and found the liquor, soberly drank the contents round the corpse of the fallen and toasted the Count with the dregs of his excellent stuff as the sun came blaz-

ing over the horizon and the station sweepers got busy.   That Dane
was hard at work an hour afterwards.

I had now some two months to while away somehow until my
hunting permit should arrive.   I took a flying trip down through
Uganda and got together a fine lot of Wanyamweze porters ready
for the hunting when it should begin.   I took sixty of these boys,
as I was pretty confident of getting the permit, and quite confident
of getting elephant, anyhow.   I arrived back at Lado and was glad
to hear from the Treasury man that he had the permit for me all in
order.   He pointed out to me that the permit stated that the hunting of elephants was not to begin until the middle of May.   It was
then March, and here was I with a large safari and everything ready
to begin.   I was wondering what to do about it when whom should
I see but my friend the Treasurer.   I pointed out my difficulty,
which he quite saw.   He said it was unfortunate, very, shaking his
head and looking thoughtfully away.   The true significance of this
pretty gesture was lost on me at first, and he had to put it pretty
broadly to me that, if he were squared, it would be possible to begin
right away.   I did not do so, and thereby made a bitter enemy.
One of the considerations dissuading me from oiling this gentleman's palm was that it seemed to me that, if I squared one, I should
have to square all, a somewhat too costly business.

Passing over to the English side of the Nile, I occupied myself
as well as I could obtaining my two elephants allowed on my
Uganda licence from the sporting herd of cow elephant which then
haunted the Gondokoro region.   This cow herd was even then
notorious for chasing travellers on the Nimule-Gondokoro road, and
had killed several natives and a gun-bearer of the D.C. who was
trying to scare them from some native gardens.   I fell in with them
only a few miles from the post and managed to kill two passable
herd bulls.   One of these, shot in the brain, fell upon a large calf,
pinning it to the ground in such a fashion that neither could the calf
release itself nor could I and my boy help it do so.   Nothing could
be done without more help, so I sent the boy off to the camp for all

hands. Meanwhile I waited under some trees 100 yds. from the dead bull and living calf. The latter was crying in a distressing way, and suddenly the cow herd came rushing along back to it. They surrounded it and crowded all about it while some of them made short rushes here and there, trunks and ears tossing about, with plenty of angry trumpeting. Now, I thought, we shall see a proof of the wonderful intelligence of the elephant. If elephants really do help off their wounded comrades, as is so often and so affectingly described by hunters, surely they will release a trapped youngster. All they have to do is to give a lift with their powerful trunks and the trick is done. Nothing of the sort happened. After a couple of hours of commotion and stamping about all round the spot my boys arrived, and it was time to drive off the herd. I found this was not so easy as it looked. First I shouted at them, man-fashion. Several short angry rushes in our direction was the answer. The boys did not like it, and I certainly did not want to do any cow shooting, so I tried the dodge of trying to imitate hyenas or lions. Whenever I had tried these curious sounds on elephant before it had invariably made them at first uneasy and then anxious to go away. But here was tougher material. They drew more closely round the fallen bulls and more tossing fronts were presented. As for any moving off there was no sign of it. I redoubled my efforts; I screeched and boomed myself hoarse, and I am certain that any other herd of elephants would have rushed shrieking from the spot. But nothing would move the Gondokoro herd. Even when I fired repeatedly over their heads nothing much happened, but when I pasted the dusty ground about their trunks with bullets they began to move quite slowly and with much stopping and running back. It was a gallant herd of ladies; very different its behaviour from that of a bull herd in a similar situation.

When the ground was clear we seized the head of the dead bull and with a combined heave raised it sufficiently to release the calf, but it was too late, he was dead.

Having entered my rifles at Lado and cleared them through the Douane, it was not necessary again to visit a Belgian post. So when the hunting season opened, I already had a herd of bull elephant located. Naturally, I lost no time when the date arrived. The date, that is, according to my calculations. This matter is of some importance, as I believe I was afterwards accused of being too soon. I may have begun a day or even two days before the date, but to the best of my knowledge it was the opening date when I found a nice little herd of bulls, several of which I killed with the brain shot. I was using at that time a very light and sweet-working Mann.-Sch. carbine, ·256 bore and weighing only $5\frac{1}{4}$ lb. With this tiny and beautiful little weapon I had extraordinary luck, and I should have continued to use it in preference to my other rifles had not its Austrian ammunition developed the serious fault of splitting at the neck. After that discovery I reverted to my well-tried and always trusty 7 mm. Mauser.

My luck was right in on that safari. The time of year was just right. All the elephant for 100 miles inland were crowded into the swamps lining the Nile banks. Hunting was difficult only on account of the high grass. To surmount this one required either a dead elephant or a tripod to stand on. From such an eminence others could generally be shot. And the best of it was the huge herds were making so much noise themselves that only a few of them could hear the report of the small-bore. None of the elephant could be driven out of the swamps. Whenever they came to the edge and saw the burnt-up country before them, they wheeled about and re-entered the swamp with such determination that nothing I could do would shake it. Later on when the rains came and the green stuff sprang up everywhere—in a night, as it were—scarcely an elephant could be found in the swamps.

Just when things were at their best tragedy darkened the prospect. Three of my boys launched and loaded with ivory a leaky dug-out. The leaks they stopped in the usual manner with clay, and shoved off. The Nile at this place was about a mile broad, and when about half way the entire end of the canoe fell out; it had been stuck in with clay. Down went everything. Now, here is a curious thing. Out of the three occupants two could swim. These two struck out for the shore and were drawn under by "crocs.," while the one who could not swim clung to the barely floating canoe, and was presently saved. He kept trying to climb into it from the side, which resulted, of course, in rolling it over and over. It may well be that to this unusual form of canoe manœuvring he owed his life. At any rate, the crocs. never touched him. A gloom settled on the camp that night certainly; but in Africa, death in, to us, strange forms produces but little impression on the native mind, and all was jolly again in a day or two.

After about two months' hunting it became necessary to bury ivory. The safari could no longer carry it, so a site was chosen close to the river bank and a huge pit dug. Large as it was, it barely took all our beautiful elephant teeth. Ivory has awkward shapes and different curves, and cannot be stowed closely. Consequently there was much earth left over after filling the pit, to show all and sundry where excavating had taken place. Where cattle or donkeys are available, the spot is enclosed by a fence of bushes, and the animals soon obliterate all traces, but here we had nothing. So to guard our precious hoard I erected a symbol which might have been mistaken by a white man for a cross made in a hurry, while its objectless appearance conveyed to the African mind the sure impress of "medicine." I remember that to one rickety arm I suspended an empty cartridge and the tip of a hippo's tail. That the medicine was good was shown three or four months later when I sent some boys for the ivory. They found that the soil had been washed away from the top, exposing completely one tusk and parts of the others, but that otherwise the cache was untouched. In spite of my giving to the boy in charge of this party one length of stick for each tusk contained in the pit, he returned with one short of the proper number. To convince him of this fact it was necessary to line out the ivory and then to cover each tusk with one bit

of stick, when, of course, there remained one stick over. Straight-
way that party had a good feed and set off for the pit again, well
over a hundred miles away. It never occurred to them that one
tusk might have been stolen. They were right. Through just
feeling that they themselves would not have touched anything,
guarded as our pit was guarded, they judged correctly that no other
native man would do so. At the bottom of the open pit and now
exposed by the rains was found the missing tusk.

After the hot work of the dry season in the swamps the open
bush country, with still short grass, was ideal for the foot-hunter.
The country was literally swarming with game of all sorts. I
remember in one day seeing six white rhino besides elephant,
buffalo and buck of various kinds. Then happened a thing that
will sound incredible to most ears. I ran to a standstill, or rather
to a walking pace, a herd of elephant. It happened thus.
Early one morning I met with a white rhino, carrying a magnificent horn. I killed him for the horn. At the shot I heard
the alarm rumble of elephant. Soon I was up to a large herd of
bulls, cows, half-growns and calves. They were not yet properly
alarmed, and were travelling slowly along. Giving hasty instructions to my boy to find the safari and to then camp it at the
water nearest to the white rhino, I tailed on to that elephant herd.
The sun then indicated about 8 a.m., and at sundown (6 p.m.)
there we were passing the carcase of the dead rhino at a footpace.
By pure luck we had described a huge circle, and it was only by
finding the dead rhino that I knew where I was. Throughout that
broiling day I had run and run, sweating out the moisture I took
in at occasional puddles in the bush, sucking it through closed teeth
to keep out the wriggling things. At that time I was not familiar
with the oblique shot at the brain from behind, and I worked hard
for each shot by racing up to a position more or less at right angles
to the beast to be shot. Consequently I gave myself a great deal
of unnecessary trouble. That I earned each shot will become
apparent when I state that although I had the herd well in hand by

about 2 p.m., the total bag for the day was but fifteen bulls. To keep behind them was easy, the difficulty was that extra burst of speed necessary to overtake and range alongside them. The curious thing was that they appeared to be genuinely distressed by the sun and the pace. In the latter part of the day, whenever I fired I produced no quickening of the herd's speed whatever. No heads turned, no flourishing of trunks, and no attempted rushes by cows as in the morning. Just a dull plodding of thoroughly beaten animals. This day's hunting has always puzzled me. I have attempted the same thing often since, but have never been able to live with them for more than a short distance. Although a large herd, it was not so large but that every individual of it was thoroughly alarmed by each shot. I think that perhaps they committed a fatal mistake in not killing me with a burst of speed at the start. I left them when I recognised the dead rhino, and found camp soon afterwards. The next two days I rested in camp, while the cutting-out gang worked back along the trail of the herd, finding and de-tusking the widely separated bodies of the dead elephants.

Shortly after leaving this camp four bull elephants were seen in the distance. As I went for them, and in passing through some thick bush, we came suddenly on two white rhino. They came confusedly barging about at very close range, and then headed straight for the safari. Now, it is usual for all porters familiar with the black rhino to throw down their loads crash bang whenever a rhino appears to be heading in their direction. Much damage then ensues to ivory if the ground be hard, and to crockery and bottles in any case. To prevent this happening I quickly killed the rhino, hoping that the shots would not alarm the elephants. We soon saw that they were still feeding slowly along, but before reaching them we came upon a lion lying down. I did not wish to disturb the elephants, but I did want his skin, which had a nice dark mane. While I hesitated he jumped up and stood broadside on. I fired a careful shot and got him. He humped his back and subsided with a little cough, while the bullet whined away in the distance. At the shot a lioness jumped up and could have been shot, but I let her go. Then on to our main objective.

This morning's work shows what a perfect game paradise I was then in.

Presently King Leopold of Belgium died, and the evacuation of the Lado began. As I mentioned before, the Belgians had six months in which to carry this out. Instead of six months they were pretty well out of it in six weeks, and now there started a kind of "rush" for the abandoned country. All sorts of men came. Government employees threw up their jobs. Masons, contractors, marine engineers, army men, hotel keepers and others came, attracted by the tales of fabulous quantities of ivory. More than one party was fired with the resolve to find Emin Pasha's buried store. It might almost have been a gold "rush."

Into the Enclave then came this horde. At first they were for the most part orderly law-abiding citizens, but soon this restraint was thrown off. Finding themselves in a country where even murder went unpunished, every man became a law unto himself. Uganda could not touch him, the Sudan had no jurisdiction for six months, and the Belgians had gone. Some of the men went utterly bad and behaved atrociously to the natives, but the majority were too decent to do anything but hunt elephants. But the few bad men made it uncommonly uncomfortable for the decent ones. The natives became disturbed, suspicious, shy and treacherous. The game was shot at, missed, wounded or killed by all sorts of people who had not the rudiments of hunter-craft or rifle shooting. The Belgian posts on the new frontier saw with alarm this invasion of heavily armed safaris ; in some cases I believe they thought we might be trying some kind of Jameson raid on the Kilo goldfields, or something of that sort. Whatever they thought, I know that in one case their representative was in a highly dangerous state of nerves. He was at Mahagi on Lake Albert Edward. I happened to be passing down the lake in my steel canoe. My boys and gear followed in a large dug-out. With the rising of the sun a breeze sprang up, and with it a lop on the water sufficient to alarm the boys in the dug-out. They happened to be passing Mahagi Port at the moment. I was miles ahead and out of sight. They decided to wait in the sheltered waters of Port Mahagi until the breeze should die down. They did so, and on landing were promptly seized by Belgian soldiery, made to unload my gear, and to carry it up to the fort.

Some hours later I came paddling along shore searching every bay for my lost safari. Crossing the mouth of Mahagi Port, and never dreaming that they would have put in there, what should I see through my glasses but my large dug-out lying on the beach, abandoned. I entered to investigate, but could see none of my boys about. Some natives told me they had been marched up to the fort.

Now, it was my habit when canoeing in those waters to do so with bare feet. It suddenly dawned on me that I had left my shoes with my safari. I thought it would be devilish awkward walking up to a strange frontier post in bare feet, to say nothing of the discomfort of climbing four or five hundred yards of stony path. I sat down and wrote a note on a scrap of paper to the officer in charge of the post, explaining what had happened, and asking him to send my safari on to the English side, only a few miles away. I also mentioned that I was on my way there. I wrote this note in English, as the Belgians usually have an English-speaking officer in their frontier posts. Beckoning a native, I sent my note up to the fort and paddled off. As I was clearing the bay I saw some soldiers issue from the fort, one of them waving a letter. I returned to the beach and waited for them to arrive, much against the advice of my boy, who said there was bad " medicine " about. I took the precaution to remain out a yard or two from the shore. Soon black soldiers were approaching. When a few yards from the canoe the corporal who was carrying the letter, or piece of paper, shoved it quickly into his pouch, slung his rifle to his shoulder, rushed to the bow of my canoe, saying to the others "Kamata M'zungu" in Kiswahili. This means "Catch or seize the white man."

I had been watching the whole manœuvre carefully, paddle in hand. When he said those words I knew there was dirty work afoot. When, therefore, the leader laid hold of the canoe I hit him a terrific blow on the head with my stout ash steering paddle. At the same time my boy shoved off, and there we were almost at once 10 yds. from the shore gang. Their leader was not stunned by my blow—it seems almost impossible to stun black men—and he had hurriedly unslung his rifle and was feverishly loading it. His companions were likewise occupied. The first ready raised and levelled his rifle, and before he could fire I shot him, aiming for the arm. He yelled and dropped his arm, while the others let fly a volley as they ducked and ran. I fired no other shot, but was sorely tempted. My boy and I now paddled vigorously for the open water, bullets raining around us, but not very close. I could distinguish a small-bore among the reports of the soldiers' guns; it was the white man of the fort taking a hand. I drew a bead on him and was again tempted, but managed to withstand it. Presently they got their cannon—a Nordenfelt, I believe—into action, but what they fired at I cannot conceive, for the shots came nowhere nearer than 100 yds. to us. I feel that one or two good rifle shots might have taken that post without any great trouble or danger to themselves.

I wondered now what to do about it. The whole thing was an infernal nuisance. I thought the best thing I could do was to go to the nearest English port and report the matter to the authorities, which I did; and in a day or two all my boys turned up except one. They said that when the row started down on the beach all the soldiers and the white man seized their rifles and rushed out to the heights overlooking the bay. With them went the guards detailed to look after the prisoners. When the road was clear these latter simply walked out of the deserted post, spread out, and were quickly lost in the bush. All except one, who foolishly ran down to the beach. He was shot. The others soon made their way overland and arrived safely at the English port.

After reorganising my safari I found myself heading for a new region, the country lying around Mt. Schweinfurth. Native information said elephant were numerous and the ivory large. This time I took all my sporting rifles. This meant that, besides my two personal rifles, I had five smart boys armed with good rifles. We all felt ready to take on anything at any time.

A few miles back from the Nile we found an exceptionally dense and isolated patch of forest. There was no other forest for miles around, and into this stronghold were crowded all kinds of elephant. They could not be dislodged or driven out as we very soon found on trying it. I never saw such vicious brutes. When you had killed a bull you could not approach it for furious elephant. I devoted some time to this patch, getting a few hard-earned bulls from it. Right in its centre there was a clear space of an acre or two in extent. Here, one day, I found a few cows and one bull sunning themselves. I had an easy shot at the bull and fired, killing him. At the shot there arose the most appalling din from the surrounding forest. Elephant in great numbers appeared from all sides crowding into the little clearing until it was packed with deeply agitated animals. Those that could, shoved their way up to the dead bull, alternately throwing their heads high in the air, then lowering them as if butting at the prostrate bull. They did not know my whereabouts, but they knew that the danger lay in the forest, for they presented a united front of angry heads all along the side within my view. They seemed to regard this clear spot as their citadel, to be defended at all cost. Short intimidating rushes out from the line were frequently made, sometimes in my direction, but more often not. But when I got a chance at another bull and fired, I really thought I had done it this time, and that the whole lot were coming. So vicious was their appearance, and so determined did they seem as they advanced, that I hurriedly withdrew more deeply into the forest. Looking back, however, I saw that, as usual, it was mostly bluff, and that they had stopped at the edge of the clearing. Presently they withdrew again, leaving, perhaps, 20 yds. between them and the forest edge. I approached again to try for another bull. Clumsy white-man fashion I made some noise, which they heard. A lightning rush by a tall and haggard looking cow right into the stuff, from which I was peeping at them, sent me off again. I now began to wonder how I was to reach the two bulls I had shot. I did not want to kill any of the cows, but thought that it might become necessary, especially as they seemed to be turning very nasty indeed. The annoying part was that I had seen several bulls right out in the sea of cows. Fitting cartridges between my left hand fingers and with full magazine I approached as quietly as possible, fully prepared to give anything heading my way a sound lesson. Looking into the brilliantly lit open space from the twilight of the forest, I saw over the backs and heads of the cows between us the towering body of a large bull well out in the centre of the herd. His tusks were hidden by the cows, but it was almost certain from his general mass that they would be satisfactory. Just the little dark slot above the earhole was intermittently uncovered by the heads, ears or trunks of the intervening cows, which were still much agitated. At last I got a clear slant and fired. The image was instantly blocked out by the thrown-up heads of several cows as they launched themselves furiously towards the shot. I was immediately engaged with three of the nearest, and sufficiently angry with them to stand my ground. I hoped also to hustle the herd out of their fighting mood. I had spent days of trouble in this patch of forest. My boys had been chased out and demoralised when they attempted to drive them. I myself had been badly scared once or twice with their barging about, and it was now time to see about it. My shot caught the leading cow in the brain and dropped her slithering on her knees right in the track of two advancing close to her. One kept on towards me, offering no decent chance at her brain, so I gave her a bullet in a non-vital place to turn her. With a shriek she stopped, slewed half round and backed a few steps. Then round came her head again facing towards me. I was on the point of making an end of her when a mass of advancing heads, trunks and ears appeared on both sides of her. From that moment onwards I can give no coherent description of what followed, because the images appeared, disappeared and changed with such rapidity as to leave no permanent impressions. In time the space was clear of living elephant. So far as that goes, it was my victory; but as for clearing that patch of forest—No. That was their victory. I had merely taught them not to use the clear space as their citadel.

Passing on, and climbing all the time, we reached a truly wonderful country. High, cool and with rolling hills. Running streams of clear cold water in every hollow, the sole bush a few forest trees lining their banks. In the wet season covered with high, strong grass, it was now burned off and the fresh young green stuff was just coming away. In the far distance could be seen from some of the higher places a dark line. It was the edge of "Darkest Africa," the great primeval forest spreading for thousands of square miles. Out of that forest, and elsewhere, had come hundreds upon hundreds of elephants to feed upon the young green stuff. They stood around on that landscape as if made of wood and stuck there. Hunting there was too easy. Beyond a few reed buck there was no other game. Soon natives flocked to our camps, and at one time there must have been 3,000 of them. They were noisy and disturbed the game, no doubt, but when it came to moving our ivory they were indispensable. Without them we could not have budged.

At a camp close to the edge of the great forest I was sitting on a little hill one evening. Along one of the innumerable elephant paths I saw a small bull coming. Suliemani, my faithful servant and cook, had for years boasted of how he would kill elephant if he were given the chance. Here it was, and I should be able to see the fun. I came down to camp, called for Suliemani, gave him a rifle and thirty rounds, pointed out to him the direction of the elephant and sent him off. Then I re-climbed the hill from which I could see both Suliemani and the elephant. The bull, having, perhaps, caught a whiff of our camp, had turned, and was now leisurely making towards the forest. Soon Suliemani got his tracks and went racing along behind him. The elephant now entered some long dry grass which had escaped the fires, and this stuff evidently hid him from Suliemani's view. At the same time it was not sufficiently high to prevent my seeing what happened through my glasses. In the high grass the elephant halted and Suliemani came slap into him. With two frightful starts Suliemani turned and fled in one direction, the elephant in the other. After half a hundred yards Suliemani pulled himself together and once more took up the trail, disappearing into the forest. Soon shot after shot was heard. There was no lack of friends in camp to carefully count the number poor Suliemani fired. When twenty-seven had been heard there was silence for a long time. Darkness fell, everyone supped. Then came Suliemani stalking empty-handed into camp. A successful hunter always cuts off the tail and brings it home. Suliemani had failed after all his blowing. The camp was filled with jeers and jibes. Not a word from Suliemani as he prepared to eat his supper. Having eaten it in silence, the whole time being ragged to death by all his mates, he quietly stepped across the camp, disappeared a moment into the darkness, and reappeared with the elephant's tail. He had killed it after all! There was a shout of laughter, but all Suliemani said was, "Of course."

IX

HUNTING IN LIBERIA

IN the year 1911 the search for new hunting grounds took me to Liberia, the Black Republic. I secured a passage by tramp steamer to Sinoe Town, Greenwood County, some few hundred miles south of the capital Monrovia. Here I landed with my little camp outfit and a decent battery, comprising a ·318 Mauser and a ·22 rook rifle.

Right on the threshold I was met by conditions which are unique in Africa, with possibly the exception of Abyssinia; for here the white man comes under the rule of the black, and any attempt at evasion or disregard of it is quickly and forcibly resented, as I witnessed immediately on stepping ashore. Among a crowd of blacks was a white man held powerless. His appearance seeming familiar, I had a nearer look, and was astonished to recognise one of the officers of the tramp steamer from which I had just landed. I asked him what the trouble was about, but he could only curse incoherently. Just then a very polite black man, in blue uniform and badge-cap, informed me that the officer had struck a native, and that the officer would have to answer for it to the magistrate. He was then promptly taken before the beak, who fined him 25 dollars *and the ship's captain 50 dollars*, although the latter had not even been on shore.

After this episode I began to wonder what I had let myself in for. I found, however, that my informant in uniform was the Customs officer, and extremely polite and anxious to help me to pass my gear through. He seemed to have absolute power in his department, and let me off very lightly indeed. In all my dealings I invariably treated the Liberians with the greatest politeness, and I was invariably received in the same way.

As soon as I had got clear of the Customs I looked out for a lodging of some sort. There were no hotels, of course, but eventually I found an Englishman who represented a rubber company. He very kindly put me up. I found that my host was the only Englishman, he, with a German trader, comprising the white community.

My host, whom I will call B., was much interested in my expedition into the interior. He told me frankly that I would have a devil of a time. He said that the jurisdiction of the Liberians extended inland for about ten miles only, and beyond that the country was in the hands of the original natives. These were all armed with guns and a few rifles, and were constantly at war with each other. This I found to be true.

As I was determined to penetrate and see for myself, he advised me to call on the Governor; also that I should take suitable presents to him. I resolved to do so. On my friend's advice I bought a case of beer and a case of Kola wine, the Governor, it appeared, being very partial to these beverages mixed. He told me that if I pressed a golden sovereign into his hand I should get what I wanted, *i.e.*, a permit to hunt elephant.

I had to engage servants, and B. said I could either buy them or hire them. He explained that slavery was rampant. Whenever a tribe in the interior brought off a successful raid on their neighbours the captives were generally brought to the coast and there sold to the Liberians, themselves liberated slaves from the United States of America. Alcoholism was so prevalent and widespread and had reached such a pitch that scarcely any children are born to the Liberians proper, in which case they buy bush children and adopt them as their own.

B. was going to a dance that night, and asked me if I would care to go with him. I was anxious to see what I could of the people and agreed to go. Later on I was surprised to see B. in full evening dress. He explained that everyone dressed. Now, as I had not brought mine, it was very awkward. But B. said it would be all right. As we were changing, a fine buxom black girl burst into our house and marched straight upstairs to B.'s room, throwing wide the door. There was B. with his white shirt and nothing else. I closed my door, but could hear the lady engaging B. for some of the dances. She then asked for the white man who had arrived that day, and then my door was thrown open. I was far from dressed myself, and something about my appearance seemed to tickle the lady immensely, for she went into peals of the jolliest laughter. She spoke English with a strong American accent, as nearly all the Liberians do. She made me promise to dance with her that night, in spite of my protests that I could not dance at all. She turned the place upside down and then departed. I hastened to ask B. what kind of dances they had, and he told me they liked waltzing best.

After dinner we sauntered off to a large barn, where a musical din denoted the dance. Here we found a fine lay-out. Lavish refreshments, chiefly composed of cakes, cold pork, gin and beer, were provided for all. Everybody was very jolly, and they *could* dance, or so it seemed to me. The girls were nearly all in white or pink dresses, but not very *décolleté*. A tall coal-black gentleman in full evening dress was master of ceremonies, but introductions soon became unnecessary. Round the refreshments gathered the old men, some in frock coats of a very ancient cut, others in more modern garments. I was hospitably pressed to drink. The musicians drank without pressing. Everybody drank, women and all. What added zest was the fact that *the fines inflicted on the steamer captain and his officer paid for the feast.* German export beer and Hamburg potato spirit were then only a few pence per bottle, consequently the dance became a debauch, seasoned drinkers though they were. The din and heat became terrific. Starched collars turned to sodden rags and things indescribable happened. Thus ended my first day in the Black Republic.

As notice had been sent the Governor of my intended visit, and I had bought the necessary beer and Kola wine, next day I set off to visit him at his residence, some little way out of town. Bush, with clearings planted with coffee, describes the country between the town and the Governor's residence, itself situated in a large coffee plantation. The house was of lumber construction and two storeys high, well built, and the largest I had yet seen. I marched up, followed by B's two boys carrying the present, to the front door. I was met immediately by a splendid-looking old black, very tall, very black, dressed in a long black frock coat, high starched collar and black cravat. With snow-white hair and Uncle Sam beard and accent to match, he received me in a really kind and hearty manner. I must confess that I felt rather diffident with my two cases of cheap liquor in the background, while I fingered a few hot sovereigns in my pocket. However, the bluff old fellow soon put me at my ease. Seeing the stuff out there on the boys' heads, he beckoned them in, helped them to lower their load, shouted to someone to come and open the boxes, sent the boys in to get a drink, and ushered me into his sitting-room, all in the jolliest manner possible. Here we talked a bit, and then I told him what I had come for. A permit to hunt elephant! Ha! ha! ha! he roared. Of course I should have a permit to hunt elephant. He wrote it there and then. Would I stop for dinner? I said I would be delighted. Then we had beer and Kola wine mixed until lunch was announced. Then the old boy took off his coat and invited me to do likewise. I did so and followed my host into the eating-room. Here was a long trestle table laid for about twenty people—white tablecloth, knives, forks, etc. As we seated ourselves, in trooped enchanting little black girls, all dressed neatly in moderately clean print dresses, with arms, necks, and legs bare. And then Mrs. Governor appeared with some larger girls. After shaking hands we all sat down to a very substantial meal. It was perfectly charming. Everyone was at ease. The old man was an excellent host and the old lady just as good a hostess. Conversation never flagged. The old man was full of his brother's doings. It appeared that his brother was a lazy, good-for-nothing fellow, who would let his cows stray on to his neighbours' plantations. My host had repeatedly remonstrated, but without effect. So that morning, having discovered some of his brother's cows meandering about the plantation, he had gone straight for his shot-gun and had rendered at least one incapable of further depredations. This act had, it appeared, stirred the brother profoundly, but in an unusual way, for he could be heard for miles bawling religious songs from his bedroom window. Whenever there was a lull during lunch we heard the monotonous chant, which appeared to amuse my host immensely.

All the little girls were called their children, but I subsequently found that the old couple were quite childless, and that these were bush children from the interior and were now adopted.

My host told me that he had been a slave in the Southern States; he said he could remember well being flogged. He said that elephant were numerous in the interior, also bush-cow (the little red buffalo), leopard, and the pigmy hippo. As regards the tribes, he laughed and said that they were a rough lot. He said that Liberia was almost continually at war with them. In this connection I heard afterwards that the bush men had been down on a raid to a neighbouring town. They had seized, stripped, and tarred and feathered the Governor, raided and carried off all the liquor in the trading stores, and enjoyed themselves generally.

Altogether, Liberia was, at the time of which I write, about the funniest show it has ever been my lot to see. When they set up their Customs to levy import duty on spirits, etc., they soon discovered that an extensive and very lucrative trade in smuggling started up. Steamers used to draw in close to the coast and sell for spot cash and gold dust whole cargoes of gin, gunpowder, caps, and articles of general trade. Natives would put off in their canoes in clouds, and in a very short time the cargo would be sold on deck and landed. In order to stop this the Republic bought a second-hand steam yacht which had originally belonged to King Leopold, I believe. For the following account of the doings of this navy I am indebted to B.; for its accuracy I cannot vouch.

According to B., then, the yacht was armed with a light gun and some machine guns. The crew were all blacks, with the exception of the captain, who was an Englishman. This Englishman was admiral of the fleet, captain and commander all in one. Evidently his gunners were so bad that he found it necessary to fire the gun himself whenever it had to be fired. As his salary was never forthcoming when due, he used to take it out of the fines he imposed on ships caught in the act. That he was energetic is shown by his first encounter with a smuggling ship. This happened to be a German, well inside the three-mile limit. The Liberian navy signalled her to stop. She disregarded this and carried on. The admiral jumped to his gun and let fly a shot across her bows. She still carried on. So then the admiral let rip and carried away a part of her bridge with the first shot. One can imagine the guttural curses and funk on that German bridge. Nothing more was needed, she hove to. The game ceased to be so popular after this encounter. Smuggling by the ship-load was stopped. Passing through the French West African port, Dakkar, some time after my visit to Liberia, I saw the Liberian navy—a beautiful little craft—lying at anchor. In answer to my enquiries I was told that she had been in dock for repairs, that the bill for these amounted to some £600, that the Republican Treasury had been unable to meet it, and that the repairers refused to let her sail until it was met. How long she remained there I cannot say.

With the acquisition of the hunting permit and the hiring of some lads from the interior, I was soon ready for the road. For ten miles or so we passed through lazily-kept coffee plantations, mostly worked by slave labour. The coffee is excellent, but produced without system. After this we began to rise gradually through virgin forests, with no inhabitants. Our road was a mere footpath. There were no flies, which was pleasant. Throughout the forest country there were neither flies nor mosquitoes, in spite of the dampness.

The first night we camped in the bush, where there were three huts. In one of these huts there lived a sort of " medicine " man. I got hold of him and asked him about my prospects of finding elephant. He was the most wide-awake business man I had met since leaving London, for he at once offered to make such "medicine" as would lead to my killing elephant with large tusks in great numbers. I told him to fire away, but before doing so he asked what I would give him. I promised that if I got large tusks I would give him a case of gin. He was delighted, but wanted a few heads of tobacco added. This was also agreed to. He said I might consider the whole thing arranged. Then he asked me if I would care to buy gold dust. I said yes. He then produced a tiny skin bag of the stuff. I scoffed and said that I could not be troubled with quantities so small. Turning indifferently away, I was about to leave him, when he said he had some more. He produced more of it, little by little, until there was perhaps £80 worth. Then I became more interested and asked him what he wanted for it. Gunpowder came the answer at once. I told him I had none. When he had brought himself to believe this he said he would exchange it for an equal weight of golden sovereigns. Had his stuff been pure this "trade" might have shown a small profit; but as it was obviously not so I, of course, refused to buy. As a matter of curiosity I bought a pinch of his dust and subsequently found that it contained about 25 per cent. of brass filings. There were certainly no flies on that magic-monger.

To his business of making medicine this hoary old rascal added the, perhaps, more lucrative one of slave dealing; for when I had retired to my camp-bed my boy came to tell me that the medicine man wished to see me. I told the boy to tell him to go now and come in the morning. The answer came that he wanted to see me very particularly. He was let in and came with a pleasant-looking young native girl following. She carried a small calabash, which the old man took from her and gave it to me, saying it was a present of honey. The girl remained kneeling and sitting on her heels. The old ruffian kept leering at her and then leering at me. He wished to sell her.

As we expected to reach the first village of the bush people that day, we were off early in the morning. As a rule, in forest country it is as well not to start too early. Until ten or eleven o'clock the bush bordering the narrow native trails is saturated with moisture and remains wet even after the passage of several people; then there is no sun to contend with, as in open country.

On the way we saw monkeys of several kinds and tracks of bush-buck and bush-cow. Hornbills were common and various kinds of forest birds. The country was in ridges, heavily wooded, with running streams of clear cold water in the hollows. Here and there could be seen scratchings where natives had been looking for gold. The whole of this country is auriferous, I believe. The gold is alluvial, and the particles widely separated by dirt; too widely for Europeans, I expect.

Late in the afternoon we arrived at the village. They knew of our coming, and the headman met us with a crowd of his people, and jolly independent in manner they were. Among the crowd there was quite a sprinkling of trade guns of the percussion cap type. Almost immediately I was shown to the hut allocated to travellers, and very grateful its shade and coolness were after the long and hilly march. Water and firewood were brought, and the cook got busy. The construction of the huts was new to me and quite excellent. The floor of the hut was raised some four feet off the ground and consisted of stout bamboo mats tightly stretched over poles. As the mats were rather loosely woven, all dirt and water simply fell through to the ground. If a bath is required you squat on the floor and dash the water over yourself; it all runs through and soon dries up again. Then the mats, being springy, make a most excellent bed. Vermin are absent. One is obliged to have one of the huts, as the bush runs close up to the villages, leaving no room for a tent, besides which the ground is so damp as to make a floor well off the ground desirable.

After refreshment I called the headman and told him I had come to hunt elephant. He asked to see my rifle. I showed it to him, my ·318. He smiled and said it would not do, peering into the small muzzle. He called for his own to show me, a huge affair, muzzle-loading and shooting a long wooden harpoon with an iron head heavily poisoned. But, he said, my rifle might do for bush-cow, of which there were plenty near at hand. He asked me if I would go after them next morning. I did not wish to a bit, but I thought it might be as well to create a good impression by killing something, so I promised to try. He then left me, and presently a nice present of food, a couple of fowls and eggs, arrived.

On the morrow I left for the bush with some local guides. We soon found fresh bush-cow tracks and took them up. They led through a lot of deadly thick stuff, wet and cold. The guides made such a noise that I thought any bush-cow that allowed us near enough to see them would have to be both sound asleep and deaf; and so it turned out, for presently we heard them stampeding through the bush. I gave it up at once, and consoled the natives by promising to kill some monkeys for them on the way back, which I had no difficulty in doing. Arrived back in the village, I gave the headman a couple of monkeys and some tobacco in return for the hospitality we had enjoyed. Then we set off forward for the hunting grounds. We had a set-back about half way, as our guides deserted us, saying they were at war with the people we were going to. This is always awkward in Africa, for the paths are so misleading. There was nothing for it but to trust to luck and push on.

After some miles of chancing our way along we saw a native on the path. As soon as we saw him he saw us and dived into the bush, trailing his long gun dangerously behind him. The alarm was out, and it was imperative to arrive at the village before anything could be organised. I gave my rifle to a boy to carry and on we went. Luckily the village was handy, and we marched straight into the middle of it and sat down, the natives, who had been having a pow-wow, scattering right and left. This is always a very disconcerting thing for natives; they seemed quite lost to see what they had regarded as an enemy an instant before sitting quietly right in the middle of their town. It is necessary on these occasions to suppress any signs of nervousness on the part of one's followers, which is not always easy. When this is done and there is no flourishing of lethal weapons I have never known it to fail. In a short time up came the headman, in an awful funk, but outwardly composed. He demanded of me what I wanted. I said, " Sit down !'' He continued to stand. I told one of my boys to bring a mat, and beckoned the headman to sit down. He did. Then I told him why we were there, and that if they showed us elephant they should have the meat. He went away and had a talk with some of his men, who had returned from the bush. I noticed that nearly all of them were armed with guns. Presently he came back and led me to a hut. I got the thing made habitable, and the usual procedure of peaceful travellers went on. No notice was taken by us of anyone, and presently the native women began to be once more visible, a pretty fair indication that no hostilities were intended, for the moment, at any rate. In an hour or two the headman came in most cordial mood. He had been pushing enquiries among my boys, I knew. Apparently all was well. He said I could not have come to a better spot for elephant, or to a better man than himself. He presumed that I had heard of him ; he seemed to think that London must be ringing with his prowess. I did not tell him I had never heard of him ; I merely smiled.

His news was most inspiring, although I knew enough of Africans to discount 75 per cent. of it. He said the bush was full of elephant. I decided to try next day for them, and told the headman so. He laughed and said we would have to sleep some nights in the bush and that food would have to be taken. Therefore, the following day was devoted to preparing food for the journey. In the evening I warned the people that I was going to fire, and showed them the penetration of a modern rifle with solid bullet. I chose for this purpose a certain white-barked tree, the wood of which I knew, from former trials, set up less resistance to the passage of a bullet than that of other trees. This particular tree was very thick, and I hoped the bullet would not fail to come out on the other side. It traversed it easily, to my relief and the astonishment of the natives, who came in crowds to see the exit hole. Of course, none of their guns would have looked at it. It is just this kind of childish little thing that impresses Africans, and when done quietly and indifferently enough is most useful. In this case the effect was doubled by the fact that in their mode of waging war the taking of cover behind trees was more than half the game. Luckily, no one was sufficiently acute to ask me to fire through some of the smaller but much tougher trees. They began to think that my rifle might kill elephant after all.

On the morrow we stored our heavy loads in the headman's hut and left for the bush. I took my camp-bed, and a ground-sheet which could be slung on a stick over it when it rained. These, with some plain food and 200 rounds of cartridges, comprised the loads, and, as we had plenty of followers, each man was lightly laden.

After passing through some plantations we were almost immediately in the virgin forest. We trekked hard all that day without seeing anything more interesting than monkeys and forest pig, but on the following day the country began to show signs of game. Bush-cow tracks became common, and we crossed several elephant paths, but devoid of recent tracks. This day I saw for the first time the comparatively tiny tracks of the pigmy hippo. In one place quite a herd of them had passed in the night. I gathered from the natives that they sometimes remained throughout the day in the dark pools of the smaller forest streams, but that usually they passed the day-time in the larger streams, when they would come up to breathe under the overhanging banks, only the nostrils emerging from the water. The reason for this extreme shyness appeared to be that the natives possessed firearms, the animals were quite defenceless, and the price of meat was high in all this stockless country. There exists such a dearth of flesh food that cannibalism is practised. Towards evening we reached a stream, on the bank of which it was decided we should camp. While a clearing was being made someone spotted a python coiled up on a rock a few feet out in the stream. They called me to come and shoot it. I ran up with my rifle to do so, and arrived just as the great snake was beginning to uncoil itself. First its head came, more and more of its body uncoiling behind it until the head reached the shore, the body bridging the space between it and the rock, where there still remained several coils. It landed in face of us, and I was waiting till enough of it had reached hard ground before firing. Meanwhile the boys, who had been clearing bush, rushed up with their slashers and attacked the huge serpent vigorously. It appeared to make no attempt to defend itself and was soon disabled by a few dozen blows on the head and neck. Although dead, the body continued to writhe with great force as it was being cut up into sections. All the natives were in high glee at securing so much good food. They said it was very good to eat, and certainly the flesh looked all right. When cooked, it became as white as boiled cod and seemed to lie in layers in the same way. The python was about 16 ft. long and contained the almost digested remains of one or more monkeys.

As I had killed two or three monkeys for them during the day the boys had a splendid feast with the python added. I noticed that they ate the python and roasted the monkeys whole to carry forward cold. I gathered that elephant might be expected next day.

It poured hard most of the night, and it was quite cold. Luckily, the forest was a splendid wind break, and but little rain reached my snug camp-bed. The boys made little shelters with under-bush, kept the fires going and ate python all night.

As soon as we were warmed up a bit next morning we started. Now, when the bush is wet and the cold of the early morning is still on, it is very hard to get a native to go ahead. Being naked, they come in for a shower bath every time they touch a branch. They simply loathe it. With difficulty one will eventually be pushed in front, but in a very short time he will pretend to have a thorn in his foot or some other pressing reason for stopping, and another has to be pushed forward. This continues until things heat up with the heightening of the sun. Not that you can see the sun when in this kind of forest; but, somehow, its heat rays penetrate the dense roof of foliage, although quite invisible.

We soon reached a lot of fresh elephant tracks. I examined them carefully, but could find no bull tracks at all. I could not even find one moderately big cow track. I was puzzled. All the tracks appeared to have been made by calves and half-grown animals. The boys were very pleased with them, however, and when I said I was not going to follow such small stuff they assured me that the smaller the track the bigger the teeth. This belief I have found to be common all over Africa, not only among native hunters, but also among whites. In my experience it has failed to stand the test of careful observation. But it is so widely held and so firmly believed in that it may be interesting to state the conclusion I have arrived at after very many opportunities of testing it. It is, of course, merely one man's experience, but I give it for what it is worth.

Very large and bulky elephants *appear* to carry small tusks. Why they appear small is this: A tusk reaches a great length and a great lip diameter in a comparatively small number of years, but is very hollow and weighs light. At this stage the bearer is still young and slim, as with man. Therefore, his *tusks* look enormous in proportion to his general bulk. Therefore, however, his tusks gain but little either in length or girth, but the hollows fill up more and more with the decades; while his body continues to fill out, he stops chasing the cows, takes less and less exercise, becomes bulkier and sourer in the temper, suffers from gout, for all I know, gets a liver—for I have found them diseased in very old elephant—and now his tusks look small in proportion to his general size. To bear me out I would point to the enormously heavy tusk in the Victoria and Albert Museum. It is only some 9 ft. long and only just over 24 ins. diameter, yet it weighs 234 lb. I have had heaps of tusks 9 ft. long and 23½ ins. in diameter which weighed a mere 100 lb. to 150 lb.

Pointing to a track which in any other country would have indicated a young cow, the headman said that its maker would be found to carry enormous tusks. I knew this was bunkum; all he wanted was meat. But it began to dawn on me that perhaps the elephant of Liberia were, like its hippo, a dwarf race. This decided me to go and have a look, so off we started.

The herd was a fairly large one and the ground soft, consequently the tracking was easy and the speed good. All were hungering for meat. What an appalling spectacle we would have been, as we raced along, for wise, calm, judicious eyes not out for blood—the natives all eager, searching the ground for tracks here and there like hounds on the trail. Some, more enterprising, chancing ahead to find the trail. A slap on the thigh signals this to the more tardy, while the pale-skinned man rests at the checks, the better to carry out his deadly work when that should begin. Watch him peering furtively through the bush in all directions, for human eye cannot pierce the dense foliage. Far better good ears than good eyes in this kind of country. Watch him during the checks listening. He imagines that those terrific vibrations his dull ears faintly gather may be caused by his quarry. How stupid he is to continue thinking so when surrounded by living evidence that it is not so, for not one of the native men has paused even for a second; they know monkeys when they hear them.

All the same, these were not ordinary "monks," they were chimpanzee, a whole colony of them. They were very busy gathering fruit, and I pointed my rifle at one huge old man "chimp." Like a flash my natives disappeared, and with such a clatter that the chimps heard and also disappeared. I had had no intention of firing, but I almost began to believe that I must have done it, so rapidly had the stage cleared. However, up came the headman, relieved that the chimps had gone. I asked him what was the matter. He told me then that chimps when in bands will attack if fired at. I don't believe it, but I am glad to say I have never tested it. They looked such jolly old hairy people.

After this we pushed along faster than ever, for the day was getting on. The quarry led us in every conceivable direction. Had I got lost or had my natives deserted me, I could not have found my way back to the village at all. The sun's position did not help, it being invisible. A compass would not have helped unless a kind of rough course had been jotted down with the distances travelled between changes of direction.

Towards evening I began to think that it was a rum go. I could see no reason why the elephant should travel so : food appeared to be plentiful. There were no signs of man anywhere. But the fact remains that their signs showed that we had gained but little on them during our nine hours' march. We had to camp for the night.

Rain during the night obliterated the tracks to some extent and made trekking slower. We had not gone far when the unexpected happened. The natives all stopped, listening. "Only monks," I thought. Wrong again, for it was elephant this time. They must have wandered round back on to their tracks, and we happened along just in the nick of time to hear them crossing. Had we been a few minutes earlier we should probably have had another day's hard going for nothing.

Some of them were quite close, making all the usual sounds of feeding elephant. The sighs, the intestinal rumbles, the cracks, the r-r-r-r-ips as they stripped branches, the little short suppressed trumpet notes, the wind noises and the thuds of flapping ears—all were there.

Now, leaving the boys, I approached alone. It was astonishing how thick the stuff seemed. I was certainly very close indeed to elephant, but nothing could I see. I started through some bush, came out sure of seeing something—and did so *when I lowered my eyes*. I had completely forgotten my idea about these being dwarf elephants, and had been unconsciously peering about for a sight at the elevation of an ordinary elephant's top parts; whereas here I was looking straight into the face of an elephant *on a level with mine* and only a matter of feet between us. At first I thought it was a calf, and was about to withdraw when I noticed a number of animals beyond the near one. All were the same height. None stood over 7 ft. at the shoulder. Their ivory was minute. I withdrew to think it over calmly. I met the headman, much too close in, and cursed him soundly. I said there was no ivory and that I was going to look for a bull among the main body, and that he had better keep well back. I was intensely annoyed at his pressing up like that and also with the appearance of the elephant. I was not so interested in the natural history point of view then as I would be now, and the fact that these elephant were as out of proportion to the ordinary elephant as the pigmy hippo is to the ordinary hippo merely irritated me.

Circling round the lot I had first seen, I got up to the bigger herd, searching vainly for a bull. I had now more leisure to examine the beasts and to compare them one with another. I soon spotted what should have been a fair herd bull, judging by the width of his forehead and the taper of his tusks, but he stood scarcely 6 ins. higher than the cows about him. His tusks were minute, but yet he had lost his baby forehead and ears, and looked, what in fact he was, a full-blown blood. I shot him. But here again I was at fault. I took a calm, deliberate shot at his brain, or rather where I thought his brain ought to be, and where it would have been in any decent elephant. But it was not there. Whether or not he was a brainless elephant I cannot positively say, for I killed him with the heart shot. But I am inclined to give him the benefit of the doubt, because I subsequently found out where others of his race kept their brains, and their situation in the head was not that of an ordinary elephant's. The ears were also different, although this is a poor distinction upon which to found a pretension to difference of race, for ears differ all over Africa. Then, the tail hairs were almost as fine as those of giraffe. As regards bulk, I should say it would take six of them to balance a big Lakka elephant.

I was thoroughly disgusted, but the boys were jubilant. *They* thought he was enormous. I said that I could not think of hunting such stuff. The tusks looked about 10 lb.—when weighed afterwards they scaled 15 lb. each, being shorter in the hollow than I had guessed them. " Well," I said, " if all your elephant are like this, I shall have to pull out." Then came some more surprises. They said all the " red " elephant were the size of the one I had just killed, but that the " blue " elephant were much bigger. " And where were the ' blue ' elephant to be found ? " I asked sarcastically ; for I thought all this just the usual bosh. " There were not many," they said, " and they never mixed with the ' red ' ones, but they were huge."

" And how big were they ? " I asked. " As high as that," pointing with their spears to a height of about 11 ft. or 12 ft. After all, I thought, it might be so, more especially as I had seen a pair of tusks of about 25 lb. each on the " beach "—as a shipping port is always called in West Africa—which were reputed to have come from this country. We then camped by the dead elephant, and the business of cutting and drying meat on fires began.

In a way, the smallness of the elephant helped me, for the meat was soon all cut into strips and hanging over fires, and the boys were eager for more. Therefore I had no difficulty in getting some of them to go with me the next day to look for the so-called " blue " elephant. I thought that if these were as big as the natives said they were, they were probably wanderers from the interior, where I knew normal-sized elephant lived, having hunted them in the hinterland of the Ivory Coast.

We hunted all that day without success, but I saw the old tracks of an ordinary elephant. These the boys said were made by a " blue " elephant. We returned, after a long day, to the meat camp. The headman announced his intention of accompanying me on the morrow, as his women would arrive that evening and would take charge of the meat. Now, here is a curious thing about Africans. If one acquires, say, a lot of meat, he tries to get it into the charge of his wives as soon as possible. While he remains in possession everybody cadges from him : friends, relations, everybody of similar age, the merest acquaintances, all seem to think that he should share the meat with them. But once the meat is handed over to his wife it is secure. Whenever anyone asks for some he refers them to his wife. That ends it, for nobody will cadge from a woman, knowing, I suppose, that it would be hopeless, for if the wife were to part with any she would be severely beaten by the husband. Yet that same husband, while still in charge of the meat, cannot refuse to share it.

With this in view, the headman had sent a runner to the village to bring his women to the elephant shortly after death, and in the night of the second day they arrived. Our rather dismal little camp became quite lively. Fires were lit all over the place, and everyone was extremely animated. When natives have recovered from the effects of their first gorge of meat they become very lively indeed. If they have a large quantity of meat, requiring several days to smoke and dry it, they dance all night. The conventional morality of their village life is cast off, and they thoroughly enjoy themselves.

Early on the following day we were off for the big elephant. About twenty natives attached themselves to us. We wandered about, crossing numerous streams, until someone found tracks. If they were small I flatly refused to follow them. Late in the afternoon a real big track of a single bull was found. It was quite fresh and absurdly easy to follow. We soon heard him, and nothing untoward took place. The brain was where it ought to be, and he fell. As I anticipated, he was a normal elephant, about 10 ft. 10 ins. at the shoulder, with quite ordinary tusks weighing 31 lb. or 32 lb. The boys thought him a monster, and asked me what I thought of " blue " elephant. He certainly was much more nearly blue than the little red-mud coloured ones of the day before.

As it was too late for anyone to return to the village that night we all camped by the elephant. Being dissatisfied with the numbers of warrantable bulls about, I decided to return to the village with the boys. So off we set across country. We travelled and travelled, as I imagined, straight towards the village. This was far from being the case, as I discovered when we all stopped to examine a man-trail. It was ours. We had been slogging it in a huge circle, and here we were back again. I had often admired and envied the Africans for their wonderful faculty for finding their way where apparently there was nothing to indicate it. I have never yet been able to exactly " place " this extraordinary faculty. They cannot explain it themselves. They simply *know* the direction without taking bearings or doing anything consciously. Always puzzling over this sense which we whites have to such a poor degree, I have watched closely leading natives scores of times. The only thing they do, as far as I could observe, is to look at trees. Occasionally they recognise one, *but they are not looking for landmarks.* They are quite indifferent about the matter. Something, which we have probably lost, leads them straight on, *even in pitch darkness.*

The occasion of which I am writing is the exception which proves the rule, for it is the only instance of natives getting seriously lost which has come under my observation, and that is more than twenty years of hunting. For seriously lost we were. We wandered about in that forest for three days. Leader after leader was tried, only to end up on our old tracks. Food ran out. The boys had eaten all the elephant meat they brought with them. My food was finished, but the cartridges were not, thank goodness. I remember ordering a cartridge belt from Rigby to hold fifty rounds. He asked me what on earth I wanted with so many on it. I said I liked them, and here was the time when it paid to have them. For now we lived entirely on monkeys, and horrible things they are. Tasting as they smell, with burning and singeing added, they are the most revolting food it has ever been my bad luck to have eaten.

At the end of the third day I thought to myself that something would have to be done. This kind of thing would end in someone getting " done in " with exhaustion. As it seemed to me that I should be the first to drop out, it appeared to be up to me to do something. But what? I had not the foggiest notion where we were. But one thing I knew : water runs downhill. Brooklets run down into streams, streams down into rivers, rivers to seas. Next morning I took a hand. I made the boys follow scrupulously the winding bed of the first stream we came to. It joined a larger one ; we followed that. Not a word of remonstrance would I listen to, nor would I tolerate any short cuts. At length we reached a large river, and I was relieved to see that they all recognised it. Did they " savvy " it? I asked. Yes, rather. So I sat down for a rest. The boys were having a fearful argument about something. It appeared that some held that our village lay up-stream, others that it was down-stream. They came to me to settle it. I asked the up-streamers to come out; they numbered seven. I counted the down-streamers; they numbered nine. I said: "The village lies down-stream"; and by the merest hazard it did.

The village from which I had done so much hunting and where I was so profusely "fêted" had acquired great riches with the meat I had given the people. In spite of this, or, perhaps, because of this, they showed great opposition to my going. At first I paid no attention to their protests, continuing calmly my preparations for departure, weighing and marking my ivory, etc. When my loads were ready I announced my intention of leaving on the morrow. This was wrong. What I should have done was to have kept my intention entirely to myself, then suddenly to have fallen in the boys, shouldered the loads and marched off. All would then have been well.

As it was, when the morrow came the boys did not. They could not be found. I could not move my loads without them.

I found the headman, accused him of playing this mean trick, and demanded the boys. He then tried all the persuasions he could think of to get me to stay. He offered me any women I fancied. That is always the first inducement in the African mind. Slaves, food, anything I wanted if I would only stay.

I got angry and cursed him and threatened to shoot up the town. He said quietly that the king was coming and I could talk to him.

Meanwhile I had to wait. I was simply furious. The suspicion that they were after my ivory kept poisoning my mind. I argued with myself that they knew the value of ivory; that they knew what a lot of gin and "trade" they would get if they took my tusks to the coast. And a white man, a hunter of elephants, "done in," what would it matter? People would say: "Serve him right," probably. Then they wanted my rifle. They had seen it kill elephant with one shot. It had wonderful medicine. Curious how near we are to the primitive. I thought of shooting someone; I actually wished to shoot someone. But that would not have helped matters. Then sense and experience came to help me and—I laughed. As soon as I laughed they laughed. I felt master of the situation.

Where was the king? Drinking beer. Let me talk to him.

I sat down in front of my hut. In a short time the king arrived with an escort of some forty guns. He seated himself in front of a hut directly across the street from me. I wanted to shake hands with him, but I did not wish to take my rifle with me, nor did I wish to leave it behind me, as it was to play a part in the comedy I had thought out.

No one could reach me from the back, as I leant against the wall of the hut. Therefore I assumed a belligerent attitude from the first, demanding to know why all my boys had been taken. The old king was, luckily, still sober—it being early in the day—and very calm and dignified. When I had stated my demand he started. He said that his people had shown me elephant; that without them I could not have found them. He said his people had treated me well. They had offered me wives of my own choosing. Food I had never lacked. Elephant were still numerous in the bush. Why should I wish to desert them in this manner?

I admitted that all he had said was true, but begged to point out that I was not a black man. I could not live always there among them. White men died when they lived too long in hot countries, and so on. Then I pointed to the fact that I had never sold the meat of the elephant I had killed, although I might have done so and bought slaves and guns with it. I had given it all freely away to him among others; and now when I wanted to go they seized my porters.

Then he tried another line. He said I could go freely if I gave him my rifle. He said I could easily get another in my country.

I turned this down so emphatically that he switched to another line.

He said, when black men went to the coast they had to pay custom dues on everything they took to or brought away from it. As this was entirely a white man's custom and yet they enforced it upon black men, putting them in prison if they did not pay, he would be obliged to make me pay customs on my ivory. He thought that if he and I divided it equally it would be a fair thing. At this I could not help laughing. The king smiled and everyone smiled. I suppose they thought I was going to pay.

But, I said, there is a difference between your country and white man's country. When a traveller arrives at the gates of the white man's country the very first thing he sees is a long building and on it the magic sign "Customs." Now on seeing this sign the traveller knows what lies before him. If he objects to paying customs, or if he has not the money with which to pay, he departs without entering that country. But when the traveller reaches the gates of the king's country, he looks in vain for "customs." Therefore, he says to himself, what a very wise and good king rules this happy country. I will enter, for there is no "customs." But if, having entered the country on this understanding, the king levies customs without having a Customs House, that traveller will recall what he said about the king and will depart, cursing that king and spreading his ill-fame so that no more travellers or elephant hunters will come near him. Therefore, I ended, the whole matter resolves itself into this : Have you a Customs House or have you not? Here I peered diligently about as if searching among the huts. The whole lot, king, court, escort and mob roared with laughter.

They were not done yet, though. The palaver ran its usual interminable length. The king accused me of disposing of the pigmy hippo meat in an illegal manner. Pigmy hippo were royal game, and every bit of it should have been sent to him. I had him again with the same gag as the customs one, *i.e.*, that when he made a law he should write it down for everyone to read, or if he could not write he ought to employ some boy who could. And so on and on.

Wearied to exhaustion, I at length decided to try what a little bluff would do. I had hoped that I would not have to use it, but it was now or never. If it came off, and the porters were forthcoming, we could just make the next village, hostile to the king, before dark.

Suddenly seizing my rifle I covered the king. No one moved.

The king took it very well, I must say. I said I was going to fight for my porters and begin on the king.

He said that to fight was a silly game. However well I shot, I could not kill more than ten of them before someone got me. I replied that that was so, *but that no one knew if he would be among the ten or not.*

I had them. They gave it up. I kept the old king covered and told him not to move until the porters arrived. He sent off runners at once. They came on the run, picked up the loads and marched. I stopped a moment to shake hands. The insatiable old rascal begged for at least some tobacco. I felt so relieved and pleased at seeing my loads on the road at last that I promised him some when we had caught up with the caravan.

B. told me on my arrival at the coast that during my absence in the interior the inspector of his company had come on a visit, straight from London. He had started from the coast with a caravan of head carriers to visit another of their depots. He had been promptly arrested, carried before the magistrate and fined twenty-five dollars for travelling on the Sabbath. The fine had been demanded at once, and someone sent off to purchase gin. The magistrate knocked the neck off a bottle, took a pull and offered it to *the prisoner!*

B. said the inspector had been very haughty with the Liberians and that they were out to get their own back.

It must not be thought that they are unfriendly towards whites. If treated politely they are very nice people indeed; they will do anything to help. But they must be treated just as if they were ordinary white foreigners. I liked them immensely, and regretted having to leave their country owing to the smallness of the ivory. And so ended my dealings with the citizens of Liberia and the natives of the hinterland.

X

BUBA GIDA, THE LAST AFRICAN POTENTATE

NOW situated in the French sphere of influence can still be found a remarkable relic of the old slave-dealing days. The country goes by the name of its despotic ruler, Buba Rei on maps, Buba Gida to everyone cognisant of it. The principal town is also so called. And the whole organisation is an example of what can be done by courage, energy, force of character and extreme cunning allied to ferocity and cruelty; for the redoubtable Buba Gida, the owner—body and soul—of tens of thousands of slaves, is no scion of a kingly race. Mothered by a slave of the Lakka tribe and fathered by a Scrub Fulani of sorts, everything he has and is he owes entirely to his own ability.

In early life he left his humble home and started out into the wild no man's land with some companions of a like spirit. Slaves at all costs were what Buba Gida and company were out for. Perhaps it was mere chance that led them towards the Lakka country, whence Buba Gida's mother had been raided, or perhaps it was information from her. However that may be, in close proximity to the Lakka country they found what they were looking for—a fine country, well watered and obviously good for cattle. Pagan Lakkas and other bush tribes were in plenty within raiding distance. Their first raid set them up in labour. Their tiny camp became a village. More raids were planned and carried out with invariable success. The village became a town.

Buba now ruled supreme. By pursuing the system of " putting away " all those who obstructed him, judiciously mixed with generous treatment in the matter of women—to acquire which the African will do anything—he obtained such a power over his people that none, not even the white man, has been able to overthrow it.

I will now try to describe how my companion and I fared when the pursuit of elephants took us into Buba Gida's country. To reach this country we traversed some very rich cattle districts inhabited by Fulani, a tribe akin to the Somals. At Buba Gida's boundary we were met by some forty or fifty of his smaller fry, for it must be understood that we were simple elephant hunters and not " big " white men. Everything about us was known to Buba Gida days before our arrival at his boundary by his wonderful system of intelligence. We remembered noticing casual horsemen about our caravan ; they were Buba Gida's intelligence. From the boundary to the king's town was six days' march, and the headman of every village we slept at was under orders to escort us to Buba Rei. As each headman in turn was escorted by five or six men, all being mounted, it will be seen that we formed quite a little army by the time we got to the capital. Had we been " big " white men, doubtless we should have been several hundred strong by that time. At the end of the sixth day we were camped within sight of the mysterious city. And mysterious it certainly is, for, surrounded as it is by well-known, if somewhat distant countries, and within 120 miles of a large Government post, nothing is known of this curious mediæval city or its despotic tyrant, Buba Gida ; and yet every white man wishes to know more about it. Countless thousands of questions must have been asked about Buba Gida. He even visits the Government station Garua ; and sufficiently foolish to us he appears when he does so, for he goes with thousands of followers, women and men. Special beds and tents are carried with all kinds of paraphernalia ; in fact, anything for show. He even must buy the whole contents of the stores he honours with a visit, much of them quite useless to him.

It was not clear to us why we had to camp so near the city, so we asked why we did not proceed. The answer was that the king had ordered us to sleep at that spot. There are few remaining places in

Africa where a white man's actions are governed by a black man's wishes. Abyssinia under Menelik was one. Liberia and Buba Rei are still among them.

On the following morning we all sallied forth in our very best paint. As all the riding horses are stallions and some of them alarmingly vicious, and all of them ready at any time to bite, kick, strike, rear and prance, and, indeed, taught to do so, it is easy to imagine the scene as we drew near the capital. Right in the thick of it, in the middle of the prancing *mêlée*, on a very high rakish-looking stallion over which he appeared to have no control, was a gentleman with a very white and anxious face. He seemed to be somewhat insecurely seated on a flat saddle and appeared to be trying to do something to his horse by means of a snaffle. I know all this because I was he. My companion looked much more at ease, but I must confess I felt thoroughly alarmed lest I should fall off and disgrace the whole show. This will be better understood when I explain that all the riders except ourselves were in saddles with great high horns in front and high cantles behind. Most of them clung openly to the horns ; and besides this, their mounts were bitted Arab fashion, with great spades and a ring round the lower jaw, so that they really had control over their beasts.

Luckily, I did not fall off, and presently we halted about a mile from one of the great gates in the wall which surrounds the town. We were told we should have to wait here until the king gave the order to enter. After waiting about two hours—done chiefly to impress the people with the greatness of the king, to see whom even the white men had to wait—a mob of mounted men about two hundred strong was seen to come forth from the city gate and to approach. We now hastily mounted, and I remember having more trouble with my infernal beast. The two opposing bodies of horsemen now began to approach one another until there remained perhaps forty yards separating us. Some very impressive speeches were made. Luckily for us, the king had lent us a speech-maker, and he held up our end in a very creditable manner, judging by the

Chimps.

A COLONY OF "CHIMPS" FRUIT-GATHERING

THE "ELEPHANT CEMETERY"

THE ARRIVAL IN WEST AFRICA

If the natives were not very expert watermen, a great portion of the coast trade would cease for lack of harbours and landing facilities. White sailors are of no use for this work. It will be noticed that the natives use paddles, which they prefer to oars, except the steersman, who uses a long sweep.

SMALL ELEPHANT OF LIBERIA

THE PALAVER WITH THE KING

The boy in the foreground, interpreting, was nearly eaten by the natives, who pleaded, in excuse, that it was their custom to eat all of that tribe that they came across.

THE SILENT TOWN: VULTURES THE ONLY SCAVENGERS

OUTSIDE THE WALLS

COMMANDERS OF REGIMENTS

CHIEFS IN ARMOUR WITH ARROW-PROOF QUILTS

A FOOT SOLDIER

AN ENORMOUS MAN, FULLY SEVEN FEET HIGH, ROSE FROM A
PILE OF RAGS AND EXTENDED HIS RIGHT HAND, SWINGING
A STRING OF HUGE AMBER BEADS IN THE OTHER.

WHENEVER THE KING SNEEZES, COUGHS OR SPITS, THE ATTENDANT SLAVES BREAK INTO
LOUD WAILING.

IN BUBA REI

LAKKAS, SHY AND NERVOUS

BUBA GIDA'S ELEPHANT HUNTERS

HE DISAPPEARED INTO THE THICK STUFF

THERE HE WAS NOW FACING ME.

GALLERY FOREST AND BABOON

CAMP ON LAKE LÉRÉ

A MAN-EATER, FROM WHOSE INSIDE A WOMAN'S BANGLE WAS TAKEN

NATIVE DECOYS: BUNDLES OF GRASS, THE ENDS WHITEWASHED, STUCK ON STICKS.
SHARI RIVER

WHISTLING TEAL AND LOCUST STORKS: BAHR AOUCK

ROLLING UP HIPPO

THE SMALL CANOE UP-STREAMING: BAHR AOUCK. THE PACKAGE IS DRIED FISH.

HIPPOPOTAMUS IN THE SHALLOWS

W., IN THE SMALL CANOE, RUNS INTO A RISING HIPPO BUT DIGS HER IN THE NECK WITH HIS PADDLE AND SHE DISAPPEARS WITH A SPLASH, NEARLY SWAMPING THE CANOE.

SPUR-WINGED GEESE: SHARI RIVER

MALE EGYPTIAN GEESE IN BREEDING SEASON: BAHR AOUCK

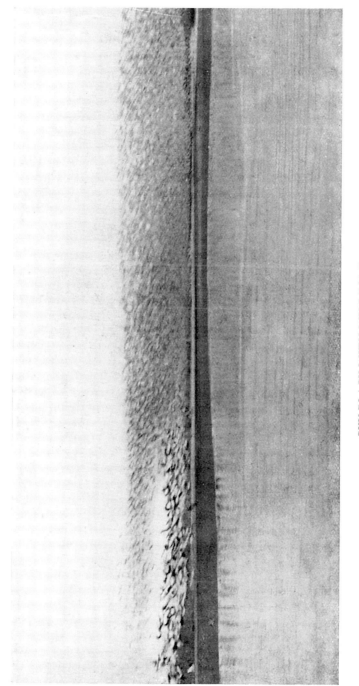

SKY BLACK WITH WILDFOWL

RHINO NEARLY HAVE OUR COOK

MUSGUM VILLAGE: INUNDATED AREA

MUD HUTS: MUSGUM

Constructed without wooden supports of any kind, and with holes in the top for exit during floods

A WATER BUCK

FEMALE WATER BUCK ON SANDBANK

DOE KOB AND CALF WELL CAMOUFLAGED

COW HIPPO AND CALF

PORTAGING CANOES

THE KILANGOZI OR HEAD PORTER WHO CARRIED THIS TUSK
(148 LBS.) FOR SIXTY-THREE CONSECUTIVE MARCHING DAYS

WORTHY GAME

IN THICK STUFF

SOME RETREATING CLEVERLY BACKWARDS AND RECEIVING THE CHARGING ANIMALS' RUSHES ON THEIR
SHIELDS, WHILE OTHERS JABBED SPEARS INTO THEIR VITALS FROM THE SIDES

DRIVEN OUT OF THE REED BEDS

As a game animal the lion affords first-class sport, and sportsmen will be glad that some protection has been given lions in East Africa. This, combined with the large stock in the game reserves, should ensure good sport for many years to come.

"A MAGNIFICENT MALE DELIBERATELY TURNED AND STOOD FACING ME."

CHASING OFF AN INTRUDER

SPOTTED!

amount of talking he did. I thought it would never end, my horse becoming more and more restive. Every time he squealed and bit one of the neighbouring horses the whole mob began playing up. I was awfully afraid he might take charge and go barging in among the knights, for such they were. Genuine knights—if not in armour, at any rate all clothed in arrow-proof quilted cloth—horses and all. On their heads the knights had bright native iron caskets. They carried long bamboo spears with iron heads. At their sides were Arab swords. Beneath the bright little caskets were faces of such revolting ugliness and ferocity as to be almost ludicrous. We had the speeches of the opposition translated to us, and the gist of them was to the effect that we were about to have the honour of entering the town of the greatest king on earth—a king who was, if not immortal, next door to it, and so on. Then we were requested to count the knights. Before we had time to count more than twenty or so we were told that they numbered 500. An obvious lie; 200 at the outside. Then we were told that each of these knights had under him 500 other knights, armed and mounted as he was. After that our attention was drawn to a foot rabble in leopard skins and large quivers full of arrows. I had failed to notice these before owing to anxiety about my steed's capers. They looked a pretty nasty crowd. Never have I seen so many hideous men together.

After the speeches we proceeded slowly towards the gates, gallopers continuously going off to report progress to the king. The wall totally encloses the town, and the gates are wide enough to allow of six men riding abreast. The wall itself is perhaps 20 ft. high and made of sun-baked mud. The thickness at the gateway is about 50 ft., but this is chiefly to impress the visitor and to shelter the guard. The rest of the wall is no more than perhaps 6 ft. at the base.

The buildings in the town are simply the ordinary grass and mud-and-wattle huts of that part of Africa, any more pretentious style of architecture not being allowed. Even pretentious or costly clothing, ornaments or style of any sort are forbidden. Music is forbidden. The drinking of intoxicants within the town is punishable by death. Outside it is allowed. No child must cry, none may laugh loudly or sing or shout. Noises of any sort are forbidden in this dismal city. The filth is indescribable. The obvious healthiness of its dwellers may be due to the fact that Buba Gida has every one of them out of it hard at work in his immense plantations every day and all day long, and also perhaps to the fact that everyone is well nourished. Where all belongs to the king who but he can make a ring in corn! Who but he can raise the cost of living! The only approach to a grumble that we heard from his people was the wish that they might own their own children.

Near about the centre of the town a great high inner wall became visible. This, we were informed, surrounded the king and his palaces. Few townsmen had ever been inside, and the king seldom comes out. Under this wall our quarters were situated, two unpretentious grass huts. In front of our huts, besides our usual ration, there were mountains of prepared foods. The things for us two white men would have fed thirty. With the food came a taster. That is a man who, by tasting everything before you, thereby guarantees it free from poison. This is the usual thing in Africa. Generally the chief of the village does it. Everything was most comfortable, and we began to think highly of our chances of coming to some arrangement with the king about elephant hunting. We were left alone for about two hours.

When the time came for our audience we were led through streets partly round the wall, and it became evident that the inner wall encircled an enormous area. It was from 40 ft. to 50 ft. high, and enormously thick at the base and in very good repair. Arrived at the gate itself, we got some idea of the immense thickness of the walls, the opening in them forming a high and very long guard-room, with huge doors of black timber at each end. This guard-room was filled with men—soldiers I suppose they were.

Arrived at the inner doors we were halted. Our guide entered alone. After some twenty minutes' waiting — again done to impress, I suppose—a slave appeared at the door and beckoned us in. He talked in a whisper and was almost nude. We entered and the great doors were closed behind us. Now we were in a courtyard with more huge doors in front of us. Another wait, but shorter. Presently appears our guide. Up till now he had seemed to us to be rather an important fellow. He had been decently dressed, at all events. But now here he was as nude as the other slaves. Another of the rules of this strange court. Everyone, barring white men, but not excepting the king's own sons, must approach the Presence almost nude, *and on all fours*. They must never look at the king's face, but must keep their foreheads to the ground. And you can bet these rules are strictly observed. Even our man—who must be in and out continually—was several shades more ashen than when outside. Our interpreter then stripped himself, and a very trembly wretch he looked. At last all was ready for our entry to the Presence. We passed through the door into a large and spot-lessly clean courtyard. Along one side ran what was evidently the reception house, a lofty building beautifully thatched, with a low verandah. Lolling on a pile of cushions on the floor of the verandah was a huge and very black negro. We walked quickly towards him, passing two nude slaves with their heads glued to the ground, while our interpreter and the functionary crawled on all fours behind us.

This at last was Buba Gida, and a very impressive creature he looked. As we drew near he got up. A fine specimen indeed, 7 ft. high if an inch, and wide in proportion. Soft, of course, but other-wise in fine condition. He extended a hand like a bath sponge for size and almost as flabby, swinging a string of enormous amber beads in the other. Having shaken hands white-man fashion, he waved us to two European chairs while he subsided on his cushions and com-menced to stoke up a small charcoal fire, throwing incense on to it. Silence had the stage for some moments and then the king sneezed. At once there was a wail from the two bowed slaves in the middle of the courtyard. This was instantly taken up and drowned by a chorus of wails from the precincts. Whenever, throughout all our interviews, the king thought we were approaching the familiar or asking awkward questions, he would sneeze or cough or spit, or even clear his throat, and there would follow this uproar from his wailing chorus.

The first question he asked was about our rifles. He was very anxious to buy them. We were overjoyed to hear that he would be pleased to help us to a good elephant country, at the same time mentioning the fact that he was very fond of ivory.

Presently the conversation drifted to fever. And here we were astounded to find that he really appeared to believe that he was immortal. He naïvely told us he was a great friend of God's, and that sickness of any sort never touched him. After many polite speeches on both sides we departed from our first visit to this remarkable man.

XI

BUBA GIDA AND THE LAKKAS

AFTER the usual interminable delays inseparable from dealings with African potentates, we were at last ready for the trek to our hunting grounds. Report had it that these lay fifteen days' march to the south. The king had been most generous. He lavished upon us food, carriers, guides, horses and even milk-cows to accompany us. He sent with us his most renowned elephant hunters, from whom I tried to get information regarding the country we were going to. The tales of countless numbers of immense elephant told us by Buba Gida himself we frankly disbelieved, as he had shown us forest tusks from his ivory store as having come from the Lakka country, which we knew lay well to the east of the great forest belt. There is no mistaking the difference between forest ivory and that from grass or scrub bush country, and, from all accounts, the Lakka country was of the latter description.

For some twelve days or so we followed narrow winding native trails through good but almost totally deserted country. Only on two occasions did we camp by human habitations, and these were merely outposts of Buba Gida's. The contrast between this well watered and healthy but uninhabited country and the miles of plantations and teeming thousands of the immediate vicinity of Buba Rei was most striking. Enquiry elicited the fact that all the former inhabitants of these rolling plains had been " gathered in " by Buba Gida, and that he was surrounded similarly on all sides by broad uninhabited belts. Game was wild and scarce. Giraffe, haartebeeste and oribi we saw in the flesh, while pig and buffalo tracks were infrequently met. Lion we heard once only. Buba's hunters told us that at one time elephant were numerous all over this country.

One of them showed us where he had killed his last one. I asked him what reward he had got from the king. He told me that the tusks were only so high, indicating a length of about 3 ft., which would correspond to a weight of perhaps 20 lbs. or 25 lbs. Continuing he said what other king would have given him so much as Baba (*i.e.*, Father), for, in spite of the smallness of the tusks, Baba had given him another woman, making his fourth, and had filled his hut with corn sufficient to keep him drunk on beer for two months. Few indeed are the Sovereigns who could have rewarded their gamekeeper in such a fashion. This man was firmly loyal to his king, and it may be of interest to enquire into this loyalty to a cruel and despotic tyrant, for it was shared by all of his subjects, as far as we could see.

Now, in this kingdom everyone and everything belongs to the king. He farms out his female slaves to all and sundry as rewards for meritorious services rendered the king. All children born as a result of these operations belong to the king, just as the parents do. It must be remembered that this is " domestic " slavery and not at all the horrible affair commercial slavery once was. There is no export of slaves, as the coming of the white man has prevented it. Domestic slavery entails upon the master certain duties towards the slave. Should the slave work well and faithfully for the master, the latter is bound to find for him a wife. The slave may, should he choose, become a freeman after sufficiently long and good service. At any time, should he possess sufficient intelligence to embrace the Mohammedan religion, he automatically becomes a freeman, for it is forbidden to enslave one of the Faith, and Buba Gida himself was a Mohammedan. To my mind the only explanation of the undoubted devotion shown by slaves to their masters is—women.

To the African a wife is everything. It is equivalent in Western life to having a living pension bestowed on you. For your wife builds your house, provides wood and water, grows your food, makes the cooking utensils, mats, beds, etc., not only for your use, but also for sale. *You* sell them and pocket the proceeds. Not only this, for she brews beer from the corn which she grows, and *you* drink it.

She drinks it and likes it, too, but naturally, you see that she does not overdo it. Then, again, she bears you children, who also work for you, and you sell the females. It really amounts to selling, although it is very bad manners to speak of the transaction as such. Marriage they call it, and dowry they call the price paid. Here again you are the lucky recipient of this dowry, and not the girl. True, you have to provide your daughter with certain things, such as a few mats, cloths, cooking pots, etc., most of which your wife makes. From all this it will be seen what very desirable creatures women are in Africa. There, as elsewhere, will be found bad wives, but where we have to grin and bear them, or divorce them, or be divorced by them, the African can send his back to her father and demand her sister in her place. This procedure is only resorted to in the case of a wife failing to bear children; any other fault, such as flirting, nagging, quarrelling, impudence, neglect or laziness, being cured at home by means best known to themselves. It is not so surprising, after all, that a man will work for the better part of his life to serve a master who will, in the course of time, bestow upon him that priceless possession—a wife.

So far our attempts to gain the confidence of our escort had always been met with great reserve on their part. In the evenings round the camp fire is where the African usually unburdens himself, but our lot had evidently been warned not to open their mouths to the white men. These orders they very faithfully obeyed until we approached the boundaries of what might be called Buba Gida's sphere of influence. Gradually they became less secretive, and we began to hear of strange doings. In a moment of excitement, brought on by the death of a fine buck, one of the old elephant hunters disclosed to me that the king's people were in the habit of raiding slaves from the Lakka country. As we would enter this country in another day or two's march for the peaceful purpose of hunting elephants, and as I hoped for the usual and invaluable help from the natives, this news was rather disconcerting, accompanied as we were by fifty or sixty slavers. In reply to the question, What will the natives do when they see us? came the cheering reply, Run like hell!

Where elephant frequent settled country, and especially where they are in the habit of visiting plantations, it is essential for the hunter to be on the most friendly terms with the natives. He must at all costs avoid frightening them. The natural suspicion with which all strangers are regarded must somehow be allayed. Generally speaking, the hunter's reputation precedes him from country to country, and, if that reputation be a good one, he is welcomed and helped. Only when tribes are at serious war with each other is there a break in this system of intelligence.

On entering the Lakkas' country, therefore, we were severely handicapped, firstly, by not having previously visited either it or its neighbours, and, secondly by having as our safari a villainous band of slave-raiders, already well known as such to the Lakkas. I anticipated trouble, not so much from the natives as from our own band of thieves. I could see that it would be necessary to take the first opportunity of impressing upon the king's people in as forcible a manner as possible that we white men were running the show and not they.

To my astonishment, on arriving at the first Lakka village we *and our raiders* were received in quite a friendly way. On enquiring into this, I found that this section of the Lakkas admitted allegiance to Buba Gida and were at war with the section further on, where we hoped to meet with elephant. Hence our welcome.

A chance to assert ourselves occurred on the first day of our arrival among the Lakkas, for no sooner had the camp been fixed up than our merry band had a Lakka youth caught and bound and heavily guarded. On enquiring into this affair it transpired that this youth had been taken in a previous raid, but had escaped and returned to his country. We had the lad straight away before us, asked him if he wished to go back to Buba Gida, and, on his saying that this was the last thing he desired, at once liberated him. He did not wait to see what else might happen; he bolted. Of course, the king's people were furious with us. We, on our part, were thoroughly disgusted with Buba Gida for having designed to carry on his dirty work under the cloak of respectability afforded by the presence of two Englishmen on a shooting trip. We had all of them before us, and explained that the very first time we found any one of them attempting anything in the slaving line we would tie him up and march him straight to the nearest military post. We let them see that we were thoroughly determined to take complete command of the expedition from now on, and had little further trouble from them. Later on, it is true, we were annoyed to find that small native boys attached themselves as camp followers to our safari. They rather embarrassed us by saying that they wished to go with us, but they quickly disappeared when their probable future was explained to them. I reckon that we must have spoiled Buba Gida's scheme to the extent of at least a round dozen of valuable slaves.

After all our trekking and the fussing with semi-civilised Africans, it was a great relief to find ourselves one day at the entrance to a village of the real genuine wild man. We had been passing through No Man's Land—as we may call the neutral zone between tribes at war—for the last few hours. As the grass was high at this season we had not been spotted, and our arrival at the village was a complete surprise. Amid terrific excitement women and children rushed for the bush, fowls raced about, dogs barked, while the young men appeared from the huts with their shields and spears, and faces dangerously scared. This is the moment of all others when anything but a perfectly tranquil outward appearance generally precipitates a tragedy. Either a native bloods his spear or arrow in the body of one of the visitors or some strung-up visitor fires his gun, when the situation gets out of hand at once. At these tense moments the appearance of a perfectly cool white man, for preference unarmed, acts in a most extraordinary manner. But duck or dodge, or get close to cover, or put up your rifle, and the thing is spoiled. There is no finer instance of this than when Boyd-Alexander went to visit the Sudan chief who had sworn to do him in. Without rifle or escort Boyd-Alexander voluntarily strolled up to this man's stronghold, knowing, as he must have done, having been warned by the Sudan authorities, that his only chance was to appear perfectly unafraid, or to avoid the country altogether. He visited the chief and, in due course, left the village, closely followed by him. In full view of the inhabitants of his village it was certainly "up to" the chief to show his hand, and I am convinced that he was on the very point of murdering Boyd-Alexander when he turned a perfectly unmoved face upon the chief and fixed him with a steady look. The chief slunk back to his village, while Boyd-Alexander pursued his way. From those who can read between the lines his description in "From the Niger to the Nile" of this little incident is an epic.

On the occasion of our first introduction to the Lakkas luckily nothing serious happened. After a few seconds of very nervous demonstrating with spears and shields, our friends-to-be rushed off in a panic, one fat youth getting a spear crossed between his legs and falling flat. As we required a guide, and as our only chance of getting one was to seize him, we secured him before he had quite recovered. He at once showed his sense by yielding quietly, although he must have been in an awful funk. This lad eventually became our voluntary guide and introducer, but for the moment we were compelled to hold him prisoner. Keeping a sharp eye on our ruffians to see that they took nothing from the huts, we passed through and finally reached the village of a man who was supposed to be the best able to show us elephant. The village, of course, was deserted, so we pitched camp bang in the centre of it. We also got our captive to shout to his friends that all was well, that we were friends and had come to hunt elephant only. This latter statement required some believing, judging by the time it took to get any answer to our overtures—which was not surprising, accompanied as we were by notorious slavers. But at last an old woman came, nosed about a bit, and left again, returning presently with the man we wanted.

I have often admired the infinite capacity of the African to take things as they come with composure, but never more so than on this occasion. Here was his village in the hands of his enemies, added to this the complication and anxiety caused by the presence in their midst of two white men. So far, his dealings with white men had been anything but pleasant—a German military expedition had passed through. Yet here he was, ready for anything that might turn up, unarmed and with a face of brass—for a day or so willing to please, but, above all, willing to speed the parting guest. Elephants? Rather! Hundreds of them, all round So-and-So's village fifteen miles further on. None here? Oh, no! They were here, but all have gone to ——. And what about those tracks we saw as we neared his village? Oh! those were made by some elephant which came from ——, but which returned to —— the next morning.

It was obvious that this eagerness to get rid of us would last just as long as we remained unwelcome; that is, until we had killed an elephant and shared the meat with the natives. After that event relations might reasonably be expected to become more cordial, provided that meanwhile we could avoid fighting in any shape or form. Now, this avoiding of fighting must necessarily depend largely on the natives themselves, for of course if one is attacked one must defend oneself. Especially so among these Lakkas was this the case, for they had no powerful chiefs whom they obeyed. Indeed, they were what my companion and myself called, loosely enough, I dare say, Bolsheviks. Every man was out for himself, and to hell with everything else. No authority of any kind was obeyed. And to this total lack of cohesion or combination we undoubtedly owed the fact that we were not attacked seriously before we became friendly with them. They had developed the art of running away to a fine point by storing their grain and beer-making appliances in the thick part of the bush, by building huts, the loss of which by fire at the hands of an enemy would occasion least labour to repair, by keeping all livestock, such as goats and sheep, tethered at a convenient distance from the village, and in many other ways assisting their one trump card—instant flight.

Few people who have not experienced it can have any conception of how effective such a " barrage " can be. You perhaps wish to traverse the country. You arrive at a village. Nobody there. You proceed along a path which seems to lead in the direction in which you wish to go. It lands you in another deserted village. Now you have to camp, and water has to be found. Sometimes in the dry season this may be miles from the camp. The drawers of water must be escorted. Then you wish to purchase food for your carriers. No one to sell it. You think to take it and leave the value in kind in its place, only to discover that no food of any kind is kept in the village. All this time not a soul is seen or even heard. You give it up and pass on to some actively hostile or friendly tribe, as the case may be.

As we appeared to be so unwelcome in this village we decided to move on the next day. The chief man of the village promised to provide us with a guide to the village where elephant were reported as visiting the gardens every night. Anxious as he was to get rid of us, we reasoned that, to attain that object, he would surely provide the guide or lead us himself. We consequently liberated our captive guide, loading him with presents and promising him mountains of meat when and wherever we should kill an elephant if he would come to claim it. He stayed around for some time, and I began to hope that he would accompany us further, but he presently disappeared.

On the morrow our reasoning about the guide was completely confounded, as white men's reasoning so often is when applied to African affairs. No guide was forthcoming, nor could the village headman be found. The village was once more completely deserted. As, however, we had been able to get the general direction from the headman before he went to bush, we broke camp and took a likely-looking path.

After much wandering from one deserted village to another we arrived in the afternoon at a large one on the edge of a slough. As usual there was not a soul to be seen, but I have no doubt that our every movement was being carefully watched. On the march some kob had been shot and a good portion of the meat reserved for any native who might venture to approach us. After we had had our meal an old man came in. He was taken no notice of by anybody— far the best way to allay suspicion. When he seemed more at his ease I gave him some buck meat. He took it and at once began to cook it, as he had seen it cut from a leg with the skin still on it. It was unlikely, therefore, to be poisoned, and besides, if he took the meat away with him he would have to share it with others. To avoid this he evidently purposed eating it in our camp.

When he had fairly got the taste of meat on his palate, I got the interpreter to work on him about elephant. At first he said there were none. We did not worry him, although we knew this to be a lie, as we had seen recent tracks that day. After some time he volunteered the information that elephant had been in the gardens the night before. I said to him that I thought I would go and kill one or two, in as indifferent a tone as I could, and that if he cared to come along he would certainly get some meat. He became quite excited then, saying he would fetch me a man who would show me where the elephant had been eating the corn in the night. Off he hurried and soon came back with several men. We were ready for them, and as they preceded us some of them ran on ahead to pick up the freshest tracks, blowing as they went their curious little signalling whistles. With these whistles they can talk over quite a distance— in fact, it is a sort of short-range wireless telegraph. We found it subsequently of great assistance, as the notes of these whistles were familiar to elephant, and they appeared not to mind them in the least.

Although the sun was already half-way between the vertical and the sundown, we judged from the air of suppressed excitement about our guides that the game was not far off. This surmise proved to be correct, for about a mile from our camp we entered a large planta- tion literally ploughed up by elephant. My companion, who was naturally the most stoical of men, showed signs of great interest. This was his first safari in real wild country, and he had never yet seen a wild elephant. All the tracks were those of bulls, and some of them were colossal. Plenty of 63-in. and 64-in. feet had been there, and one with a circumference of 70 ins. This meant that the owner had a shoulder height not far short of 12 ft. We thought that if their tusks were in proportion to their feet we had indeed struck lucky.

The elephant had evidently been visiting this plantation nightly for some time, and the damage must have appeared terrible in the eyes of the owners. Bananas had been stripped, broken off, or completely uprooted. Sugar cane ceased to exist. Much of the millet had been eaten and more trampled down. But it was the ground-nuts which had suffered most. These nuts grow in clusters on the roots of a clover-like plant and are barely covered with soil. The shell is quite fragile and cracks on the least pressure being applied. When it is remembered that the foot of an elephant covers some two square feet of ground, and that he has four of them, and that when feeding he is seldom still for long, one begins faintly to appreciate the devastating effect two or three dozen of them would have on any garden.

Wasting no more time than was necessary to unravel the tracks, we were soon hot on the trail of a large bull. This trail led us among other gardens for a time, all similarly raided. But presently we left cultivation and plunged into high bush, fairly dense in parts, with long grass in the more open places. I stopped and told the crowd of natives who had tagged themselves on to us that no one was to follow us on any account, hinting with my rifle what would happen if they did so. Then we took with us one native and followed the trail. In a very short time we heard noises ahead of us. We stopped to listen. Sure enough it was elephant. Leaving the native, we walked carefully but rapidly toward the noises. It had been arranged between us that, as I had had previous experience of this game, I was to do the shooting, while my companion picked up what tips he could. I was leading when I suddenly saw through the clearer ground-stems of the bush the feet and parts of the legs of a motionless elephant. At the same time the noises we had been approaching appeared to come from beyond this quiet elephant. A glance through the leaves revealed nothing of his body. This was awkward. He was only a few paces distant, and the wind was all over the place, as is usual in thick stuff. If we ran into him and killed him the chances were that the shot would stampede the others. And then, he might have little or no ivory, although his legs and feet were massive enough. Relying on these elephants being quite familiar with human smell, I slipped round behind him, making plenty of unavoidable noise, and so got between him and the noisy bunch. We were rewarded for this manoeuvre by reaching an opening in the bush which gave us not only a view of the noisy ones, but also a glance at our first friend as he moved off. This glance showed that he had short but thick ivory. I instantly put a shot into him and another into what appeared to be the largest among the noisy ones. Both were heart shots, as in this type of bush the lower half of an elephant is generally more clearly disclosed than the upper half. At the shot there was the usual terrific commotion, crashing trees and dust. Hot on the vanishing sterns we raced and jumped to a standstill, face to face with the first elephant I had fired at. Head on, there he stood, perfectly motionless, about ten yards away. To me, of course, he was merely a stricken animal and would topple over in a few moments ; but to my companion he must have appeared quite sufficiently grim and menacing. I dropped him with the frontal brain shot, and showed my companion the direction and elevation for this shot, and then off we raced again on the trail of the others. We soon came upon the second elephant ; he was down, but not yet quite dead. As he raised his head my companion tried a shot at his brain with his ·450, but failed to find it. I finished him with a ·318.

Leaving W. to wait for the natives, I tried on alone. I had not gone a quarter of a mile when I caught sight of a large bull elephant.

He was moving towards an abandoned plantation through nice open stuff, and had I been able to reach him before he arrived at the densely bushed plantation I would have got him easily. But he reached and disappeared into the thick stuff without offering a chance. One would imagine that so massive an animal would leave behind him a passage clear enough for a man to pass along with ease and speed. This is by no means the case; everything rises up and closes in behind him again, and the trail remains almost as difficult to follow as before. I plunged into the horrible stuff and was soon close up to his stern. All I could do was to keep close up and wait until either we reached an open patch, when I might be able to range up alongside, or until he turned so as to give a chance at the brain. The rifle cartridge is not yet invented which will rake a full-grown elephant from stern to vitals.

As I stumbled and clambered and pushed and sweated along behind this fellow he suddenly stopped, stood for an instant, then threw his head up, backed sharply towards me and to my left, at the same time bringing his front end round with a swing, and there he was now facing me. This manœuvre was so unexpected and done so swiftly —all in one movement, as it were—as to be perfectly amazing. The transformation from that massive but rather ridiculous-looking stern to the much higher head, with its broad forehead, gleaming tusks and squirming trunk, was so sudden and disconcerting that I missed the brain and had barely time to reload and fire again—this time into his body and from the hip, with the muzzle perhaps only a few inches from his hide—as he rushed over the very spot I had occupied an instant before. Whew! But I thought I had him, although I suspected I had placed my shot too low. This was wrong, for I just then heard a crash and knew he was down. He was stone dead when I reached him. It was almost sundown, and I called up the natives. W. came with them. I was very exhausted and thirsty, having done no elephant hunting since before the war, so we demanded beer from the Lakkas, who were now our bosom friends. This was soon forth-coming from the bush, and very refreshing we both found it. We had three very large elephants, which would supply everyone with meat, and we expected that it would bring the natives in from other parts with further news of elephant. The ivory was very disappointing; it was of good quality, but very short and hollow. After the death of the first elephant, runners had gone to bring up the safari to a nearer village, so that we had not the long and deadly trek so common after an elephant hunt. In fact, we had barely gone a mile when we saw the welcome reflection of our fires on the trees, and we were soon as comfortable as possible.

After a substantial meal of buck-meat and rice, I asked W. what his impressions had been like. He told me the most vivid occurred when I fired the first shot. He said it appeared for all the world as if the elephant were motionless and the trees rushing past them.

As anticipated, the Lakkas became much more friendly after enjoying such mountains of meat, to say nothing of the riddance of the marauders from their gardens. They never became of very much use to us in the capacity of carriers, and always bolted to the bush when the subject was mentioned. Even when we offered lavish payment in trade goods for the carrying of our ivory from one village to another they invariably bolted. They could never quite trust our following, I think.

We hunted elephant for some time in this country. There were numerous bull herds scattered about, living chiefly upon native plantations, and we ridded the Lakkas of a fair number, although the nature of the country was against big bags. When the time came for us to return to Buba Rei to get our canoes we parted firm friends with the Lakkas. The return journey was accomplished without incident more alarming than a poor abortive attempt by some Lakkas to spear some of our following. No one was hurt, and we were overjoyed to receive news while on the return journey that our canoes had arrived. The short rains had begun, and we had some trouble crossing some of the rivers. We could now begin the real expedition, which had as its object the ascent of the practically unknown and quite unexplored Bahr Aouck.

On our arrival at Buba Rei for the second time we again visited the king to thank him for all he had done for us. This time relations were rather frigid. To begin with, the king remained lolling on his couch when he received us. He had, of course, heard all about our refusing to allow any " recruiting " of slaves to be carried out, and I daresay he was furious with us. He remained polite but cold, and we noticed a great falling off in the presents of food, etc., which are demanded by custom. Among other things we were distinctly annoyed to find that we were classed by the king as third-class white men. To Buba Gida there were three classes of European. In the first category were French governors, French administrators, and French military officers. For these sweet champagne was forthcoming, in quantities to suit the individual importance of the visitor. Class two comprised minor French officials, important American or English travellers, scientific expeditions, surveys, etc.; these got whisky, while ginger beer was reserved for elephant hunters, clerks, or small commercial people. We were Ginger Beerites.

In spite of this we calculated what we owed the king, and paid him by presenting him with three tusks. He seemed only tolerably pleased with these. It was with a feeling of relief that we departed from Buba Rei and its atmosphere of intrigue and cruelty.

XII

THE ASCENT OF THE BAHR AOUCK

IT was from native sources that I first heard of the Bahr Aouck. While hunting elephant both to the north and south of its junction with the Shari River I had repeatedly heard of a large river. But I had noticed that whenever I tried to get a native to give definite information about this mysterious river he at once became very reserved. For some time I treated the existence of this river as being rather mythical, until I came across a vague reference to it in Kumm's book on Africa. I made more enquiries both among white men and natives, and at last I came to the conclusion that there was nothing for it but to go and see. Some accounts said it existed, some that it existed for some distance, but then disappeared into the ground ; some pooh-poohed its existence altogether, while others had it that no one could penetrate in face of the opposition that would be encountered. Another authority on the subject—he was military governor of the whole country in which the mysterious river was supposed to exist—held the view that all the remnants of the Khalifa's die-hards and the riff-raff from all parts had a kind of last stronghold on this river, and that nothing short of a well-equipped military expedition could go through. Another account said there was no water during the dry season.

All these conflicting accounts proved to be wrong. There was enough water to float a river steamer at the height of the dry season. There were no die-hards or riff-raff of any sort—indeed, there were no inhabitants at all, for the very good reason that the whole country became inundated during the wet season. And as for its disappearance into the ground, all that we who ascended it can say is that it was not doing it while we were there. The outbreak of war prevented any attempt on my part to probe the mystery. Here I might as well confess that it was not so much a desire to probe the mystery as the hope of finding some good elephant country which decided me to attempt an ascent.

Obviously some kind of water craft would have to be employed. If there was a river there would probably be sufficient water to float a canoe. At the same time there would probably be shallows where even a native canoe would ground. Native canoes are very heavy to portage, therefore it seemed to me that Canadian canoes of the " freight " type were the only means of transport holding out any hope of proving successful. Hence, when the war was over, my friend W. and myself decided to try our luck. With this end in view we ordered two canoes from the Peterborough Canoe Company of Canada to be shipped direct to Africa from New York. One of these canoes was 18 ft. by 44 ins., and carried an enormous amount of stuff, while the other was smaller. Their construction was vertical strip covered with canvas. The big one weighed 150 lb. and could be carried by two men easily. I may say at once that these canoes were the greatest success. We had with us quick-repair outfits, and whenever a hole was knocked in them we patched it up in a few minutes. As regards propulsion, they proved to be by far the cheapest form of transport I have ever had, for one's ordinary boys, cook, and gun-bearers could and did paddle and push them along against the current at a rate of twenty miles a day, and that without great fatigue, so easily do these delightful, graceful, fine-lined and efficient little craft slip through the water. Out of all our boys only one was what could be called a waterman ; the others had no previous experience whatever of canoes or water.

To reach the watershed to which our mystery river belonged—if it existed at all—it was necessary to travel many hundreds of weary miles. First 500 miles against the current. Then a land portage of eighty miles. Then a descent with the current of 200 miles, and then an ascent against the current of some 450 miles. Incredible as it may seem in these days of quick transport, this trek took four months to accomplish, and that before reaching the beginning of the unknown river. Long before we arrived there our scanty store of European provisions was finished, and we lived entirely upon the country. We had left England very poorly provided with provisions, as there were regulations still in force prohibiting the export of foodstuffs.

On our way and while waiting for our canoes, which had got sadly delayed among the shippers, we visited the native Sultan Buba Gida, as I described in Chapter X. On our return from Buba's country—where we had some interesting shooting—we found our canoes ready for us. It did not take us long to get our gear ready, and off we started up-stream for the long and arduous journey before us. We made sails and fitted masts to the canoes, as we often had a following wind, and they assisted tremendously. W. was an accomplished waterman and steered one canoe, while I steered the big one. So as to be handy to our fleet we had been camped on a beautiful sand-bank while preparing for the start, and every evening we practised the boys in paddling. When the day came, when all was stowed neatly away, we rattled off up-stream at a great pace, passing easily any craft on the river.

As our way now lay for hundreds of miles through more or less well-known country, I will merely recount the incidents of more than ordinary interest. One of these happened when we made a halt for washing clothes. One of our boys—*who could not swim*—calmly walked into a very deep and dangerously swift part of the river to recover his shirt which had blown in. To his astonishment he found that he could not keep his head above water. Judging by the expression on the face which every now and again bobbed up at a rapidly increasing distance, this—to him—curious fact did not seem to alarm him at all. The perfect fool kept grinning every time his head came out. It suddenly dawned upon me that I had seen this kind of thing before, and that the boy was really drowning. I immediately shoved the naked headman—a clever swimmer—into the river, telling him to save the lad. But long before he reached him the gallant W. had towed him to the bank, where he continued to grin foolishly.

Another was when I pipped an enormous "croc." He was floating lazily down the centre of the current when I shot him. Hit in the brain, he happened to float until some natives got their fish-harpoons into him. They towed him ashore and cut him up, and there in his inside was what I had read of in travellers' tales, but had never before seen—a native woman's brass bangle. The natives of the place claimed to know this croc. well, and even to know the name of the bangle's former owner. The finding of the bangle did not at all prevent the natives from eating the croc. In connection with the finding of bangles in crocs.' insides, a missionary we met advanced a theory that the crocs. picked up and swallowed a lot of these from the river bed. But he could not explain how the bangles got there.

Throughout this expedition W. and I lived for the most part on what we shot and on what we could buy from the natives. Almost everywhere we got whistling teal with great ease. One shot from W.'s 12-bore would usually provide enough for all hands. He seldom picked up less than five or six, and once we gathered twenty-nine from a single discharge. They were tender and fat enough to cook in their own juice, and their flavour was exquisite. They were literally in tens of thousands in some places. There were many other fowl in thousands also, but none were so good to eat as the whistlers, except the tiny and beautiful "butter-ball" teal. These were rather rare. The spur-winged goose and the Egyptian goose were also very numerous, but tough and strong in the pot. Guinea-fowl were very common, and the young ones were delicious, while the old ones made capital soup. On one occasion we heard guinea-fowl making a tremendous clatter in the bush by the river bank. We paddled over to shoot some for the pot. W. fired at one in a tree from the canoe. At the report a large lioness slunk away through the bush. This occurred on our way home, and as we were by that time satiated with lion we let her go unmolested.

Besides all the fowl there were fish in abundance. W. was a

great fisherman, and had brought a good assortment of hooks and strong sea lines. We were seldom out of fish. As soon as we arrived at the camping ground W. and the boys would bait their hooks with teal-guts or a piece of buck meat, and in a very short time either the tackle was broken or a fine fish landed. W. could never resist for long the temptation to bait a hook with a small fish of $\frac{1}{2}$ lb. or so, in the hope of catching that most sporting and excellent fish the tiger or "capitaine." It always ended in his hooking a tiger, but it also ended in the complete loss of hook and most of the line. No gear, however strong, seemed capable of holding this fish. We often admired them as they leapt feet into the air when in hot pursuit of some smaller fish. They presented such an air of activity and energy on these occasions as to make the movements of running salmon appear quite tame and slow in comparison. That they are equally good on the table we had many opportunities of testing, as we always chose them in preference to the others when buying from the natives, who catch them in clever traps. We once had a "capitaine" served up with mayonnaise and the most perfect wine ; this was when we lunched with the Governor, and a more delicious fish could not be imagined. We were told, as a tribute to its excellent qualities, that it derived its name from the fact that it was considered that no one below the rank of "capitaine" was worthy to eat it.

Time accomplishes wonders even in Africa, and at last we were actually about to enter the Bahr Aouck. We were deeply laden with foodstuffs, ready for anything that might turn up. W. had a ·318 Mauser, a ·450 D.B., and a 12-bore shot-gun. I had a ·318 and a ·22. Stacks of ammunition for these lay snugly packed in tins in the canoe hold. Then we had six "boys," all pretty expert with canoes by this time. We had these boys in splendid order. They were of no particular tribe or caste—in fact, they were all of different tribes or castes. We paid them well, but, what was of far greater importance, we kept them in tip-top condition. Living ourselves, as we were by this time, entirely upon native food, we appreciated at their correct value the many and various grains, nuts, oils, etc., and whatever we had our boys also shared. Fish and meat, millet or maize meal, rice and ground-nuts, palm oil, sim-sim oil, ground-nut meal and honey, all were to be found in the capacious hold of our cargo canoe, and all at a trifling cost. Whenever we were compelled to replenish our store of foodstuffs we killed a hippo or two, rolled it up on a sand-bank, and immediately a market would spring up.

The consequence of this high living was a state of high efficiency and contentment among the crew. As none of them had ever been with white men except the cook, who had been with a German, they were all unspoiled and all willing to do anything that turned up. The cooks were boys one day, tusk-choppers the next, canoe carriers the next, and so on. Everybody had to turn their hands to anything, and all were crew.

When, therefore, we sighted the junction of the Bahr Aouck with the Shari, against whose sluggish current we had paddled so many weary miles, we all felt keen and ready to tackle anything that might turn up. We had been careful to keep our destination secret, so that when we actually steered our canoes into the Bahr Aouck our boys had not the slightest inkling of our intention to ascend this river. All being strangers to this country they had never heard of the Bahr Aouck—or, indeed, of any other of the many "bahrs" there. But had they known the name, through our having mentioned that we were going there, it is almost certain that they would have made enquiries among the natives we had already met with, and that from them they would have received such dreadful reports as would have led them to desert rather than penetrate the unknown. Consequently, when we paddled vigorously into the swifter current of the Bahr Aouck we were all a merry crew; the boys were merry because they did not know where they were, and W. and I were merry because we did know where we were, and also because the water which bore us at that moment was obviously that of a considerable river, and we thought that if it did not split up into many smaller streams we would go far, and perhaps discover something

worth while. I do not know what W. would have considered worth
while, as he never showed feeling of any sort and he did not tell me.
Although all this was quite new to him, one would have said, on
seeing him at this moment, that he must have been exploring unknown country all his life and had grown tired of it. To me, the
moment of our entry into the Bahr Aouck was most exhilarating.
I had visions of immense herds of unsophisticated elephant with
enormous ivory ; perhaps new tribes, gold, diamonds, stores of dead
ivory waiting for someone to pick them up, new animals, water-
elephants, and a thousand and one other visions. As usual with
visions, none of these materialised.

As we poled up-stream I took soundings. There were eight feet
of water in some places, in spite of it being the dry season. For the
first few days we saw very little game. A few kob and water buck,
baboons and duiker. Once we saw some fishing natives with their
traps. They sold us some excellent smoked fish, and told us that
there was one village ahead of us, but beyond that nothing. The
next day we saw where a herd of elephant had crossed the river some
days before. Hippo now became more common, and at one place
where the river formed a large pool there must have been about a
hundred of them bobbing up and down. A mile or two further and
we came to the village mentioned by the fishermen. It was not
actually on the banks, but we knew we were close to it by the canoes
and paths. Here we camped, hoping to get some information of the
river ahead of us. This was not forthcoming to any extent. When
asked, the natives generally appeared uneasy, said they had never
been up-stream, or muttered something vague about bad people
further on. All agreed, however, that there were no more villages.
This determined us to lay in a large cargo of foodstuffs. In order to
do this I dropped down-stream to the hippo pool with the small
Canadian, now empty. I paddled to a sand-spit which stuck out con-
veniently into the pool. It was literally covered with fowl of various
kinds as we approached. From the sand-spit I proceeded to shoot
hippo in the brain, and had no difficulty in killing enough to provide

us with sufficient food for a month or two, when the meat had been exchanged for flour, etc. Hippo sink to the bottom when shot in the brain, remaining there for a variable time, depending on the temperature of the water, the stage of fermentation reached by the stomach contents, the inflation or otherwise of the lungs at the moment of death, and the state of the river bottom. Generally this period ranges between twenty minutes and one and a half hours. Shortly after the first carcase had floated to the surface the natives began to arrive. Some of these I sent off hot-foot to tell the whole village that there was meat and fat for all who should bring food in exchange. Meanwhile the carcases were towed to land and rolled up as soon as they floated. When the last had been so dealt with the cutting up commenced, and when that was completed there were already dozens of women waiting with calabashes of meal, etc., to exchange for meat. Such a feast I dare say they had never seen before. It is seldom that more than one hippo is killed at one time by native methods, except on the Upper Nile, where they have a kind of grand battue in which hundreds of canoes take part. Presently our market became very big. No sooner did the natives see the size of the chunks of reeking beef given in exchange for the various commodities than they rushed off to their homes to bring something to barter. We obtained every conceivable kind of native produce. Among the items was a canoe-load of smoked fish. This must have weighed about 200 lb. and was bartered for half a hippo. We also got some curious tobacco. Only the very small leaves and the tobacco flowers were in this particular mixture. We both smoked it regularly and became very fond of it. But it was very potent indeed, and had a far more drug-like effect than ordinary tobacco.

The slaughter of these hippo and the subsequent bartering had brought us into touch with the natives very nicely indeed, and all were most friendly. So much so was this the case that I ventured to approach one of their canoe-men with the suggestion that he should accompany us up-stream. Rather to my surprise he agreed to do so. Encouraged by this, I suggested that perhaps he had a friend who might like to go with him. He said that he thought one of his friends would go also. We were very glad indeed to have these fellows. The first was quite a youth but a good waterman, while the second was a hard-bitten man of middle age. I thought he would make a good tracker for W. when we should reach elephant country. He was not a waterman at all; in fact, he fell overboard from the small canoe—which was W.'s—so often that I was obliged to put him in the larger and more stable one.

When all was ready we pushed off, very deeply laden. All was now new river ahead of us. As we progressed day by day hippo became more and more numerous. In some places they formed almost a complete barrage across the river. Sometimes it was ticklish work steering between them. Their heads often came up quite close to the canoes, and then they stared at us goggle-eyed with astonishment. Once W.'s canoe ran its stem on to the neck of a rising hippo, the fore part being lifted clean out of the water, canting over dangerously, and then let down with a whack as the old hippo dived. They shipped a deal of water, but there was no damage done. We soon found that if we kept on the shallow side of the pools we ran less chance of bumping into them, our only danger then being from hippo asleep on the bank suddenly waking up and rushing blindly towards deep water. Had we ever had the ill luck to have been across their way, I believe they would have rushed clean into or over us.

For many days we saw no sign of elephant. Kob and water buck were fairly numerous on the banks, and whistling teal, guinea-fowl, Egyptian geese, spoonbills and egrets were common, while inland giraffe, rhino, buffalo, haartebeeste, topi, oribi, roan, and duiker were numerous. Lion were frequently heard, and W. shot a fine male on the carcase of a hippo which was pretty far gone. This hippo must have been wounded by man somewhere, as it was full grown and quite beyond a lion's ability to kill. Fish became so unsophisticated as to take anything you liked to put on a hook, and that right alongside the canoe. So tame were they that our boys used to dangle buck gralloch in the water and spear the fish which immediately swarmed round it. Why fish were so numerous I do not rightly understand. It may have been because there were no natives, who, with their gigantic traps, must destroy countless fish. A curious thing was that the enormous " crocs." we saw appeared to prefer buck to fish. One which we shot was dragging a dead haartebeeste into the water. The haartebeeste was full grown and had evidently been kept under water for some time. We often spotted these monsters lying motionless in the grass, waiting for buck to come along, I imagine. Another large crocodile whom we were tempted to photograph was taken by W. at only about 8 yds. range. He had sustained damage to one eye—the one nearest the photographer—and probably that was why W. could approach him so closely.

So far we had not met with great numbers of tsetse. But now we began to reach a very flat country which was evidently all under water in the wet season. Half submerged evergreen forests became more and more common. These cool, damp forests were full of tsetse, and in a few days we were overjoyed to find that elephant frequented them in goodly numbers. Buffalo also seemed fond of them. Had it not been for the swarms of tsetse I think we would have found these groves of evergreen standing full of elephant and buffalo. As it was they came to them only by night, withdrawing to the open bush and dry grass lands in the daytime. Only once did we actually see elephant from the canoes in the daytime, although we frequently did so by night.

One day we saw ahead of us what appeared like pure white trees. When we drew near we saw that the white on the trees was caused by a colony of egrets sitting on their nests, the surrounding foliage being covered with their droppings. A curious fact in connection with this colony was that when we repassed it on our way downstream some six weeks after, white spoonbills had taken over the nests and were busy sitting on them, while their earlier occupants, the egrets, were all over the sand-banks, teaching their half-grown progeny how to catch fish, etc.

At the time of our up-stream journey the Egyptian goose was also breeding. On every sand-bank there were scores of ganders, while the geese were hidden away in the vegetation, sitting on their nests. These we found, but always with great difficulty, so well were they hidden.

Fly and game became more and more plentiful as we journeyed on. When I speak of fly I mean tsetse; there were other flies in plenty, but they appeared of no importance beside the fiendish tsetse. We began to see buffalo now, and one day we saw where the river bank had been trampled down. As we approached it became clear that a very large herd of elephants had been there. It was soon evident that the tracks were quite recent, having been made the night before. We found a nice site for camp on an island, where our fires would not be seen by elephant revisiting their drinking place. We hoped that they would come in the night, and sure enough they did so, soon after sundown—such a splashing and rumbling, trumpeting and crashing. Lions were also busy, roaring on both sides of the river. It was a busy spot and one of our happiest camps. From it as base we hunted in all directions. And what a long way the elephant used to go in the daytime from the river. They would come to the river just after sundown when the flies were quiet. There they would spend the night, crashing the evergreen gallery-forest, plastering themselves with mud as a protection against fly on the following day, eating acres of the still green river grass, and generally enjoying themselves. It must be remembered that at this season everything a few yards back from the river is burnt up either by sun or fire. The dry season in these tropical parts is the winter of the Northern Hemisphere, in its effects upon vegetation. Instead of dying off the grass is burnt off. The grass fires wither the leaves on the trees and they fall immediately after. All temporary water, such as pools, puddles, etc., dries up. Fly desert the dry parts and congregate in myriads in the shade of the river forest. But they will follow man or beast for miles into the dry country. It is astounding to look behind one as one leaves the vicinity of the river. Behind each man there is a small cloud of tsetse; they keep about two or three feet from the ground. Each traveller keeps flicking away fly that settle on the man in front of him. It is rather startling at first to receive a hard slap on the back when one is not expecting it. Fly generally got us under the brims of our hats and, when near to buffalo, one would be bitten every thirty seconds. Lucky for us that there were no natives about with sleeping sickness. During the dry season there is not much for elephant to eat away from the river. They pick up a fair lot of tamarind fruit, dig up roots, and chew aloes and sansivera fibre, spitting out the fibre in balls. But it is on the river that they depend for the bulk of their green food and water, and, were it not for fly, they would doubtless remain there day and night.

Early on the following morning W. and I separated, he taking one bank while I took the other. I tracked a large herd back from the river for about five hours' fairly slow going, as the tracking was difficult. Dry season tracking is difficult because the ground becomes so hard, also because all the old tracks remain, as there is no rain to obliterate them.

About fifteen miles back from their drinking place there were signs of the elephant having left their huge and wellworn trails, scattering right and left into small groups, the better to find their scanty food. We saw plenty of fresh rhino spoor, but this was one of the few days upon which we did not encounter them in the flesh.

We had been disentangling the trail of a large bull and had brought it, through the scores of other tracks, right from the river bank. We were rewarded presently by sighting him by himself, wandering gently on. The country was altogether in favour of the rifle, and he had no chance. But after the shot I was astonished to see elephant emerge from the bushy parts, strolling aimlessly about, apparently quite unscared by the sound of a rifle. I went through crowds and crowds of them, getting a bull here and there. It was many years since I had seen elephant so unacquainted with firearms. They appeared to take the crack of the ·318 for the crack of a breaking tree-stem or something of that sort.

As our hunting operations were all rather similar to the above, except in result, I will pass them over and merely remark on the extraordinary numbers of rhino we met. They were so stupid and so numerous as to be a perfect nuisance. On sighting one we generally tried to avoid him by making a detour, but even then they would sometimes follow us. On several occasions our boys got into trouble with them and they had to be shot in order to avoid accidents. Once, on leaving camp for a few days' tour in the bush, we started a big cow and a bull from the river bush. They trotted away and I thought no more about them. About an hour afterwards I heard a frantic shout behind me. I looked round, and there was my boy legging it straight towards me, with our two friends of the morning close behind him. The big cow was leading and was quite close to the boy. They were all going their hardest, and really appeared bent on mischief, so I was compelled to shoot the cow and, shortly afterwards, the bull also, as he went barging stupidly about. I sent afterwards for the horns of these rhino when I thought they would be sufficiently rotten to disengage easily. The boy who went for them found the bodies in the possession of three lions, which refused to budge when shouted at. We had provided the boy with a rifle. He said that he fired it at the lions, who took no notice of it, but continued to growl at him. He then had another shot, which hit one of them. They all withdrew a little distance, when the boy had another shot at the wounded one and killed him. He said that the others remained about in the vicinity while he skinned the lion and pulled off the horns of the now putrid rhino.

Besides rhino there were many lions, some of immense size, although with poor manes. Although I knew the Athi Plains in British East Africa in the old days, and many other parts of Africa, I have never seen such numbers of lions. I believe I am correct in stating that every carcase of elephant that we shot during the entire time was found in the possession of at least one lion when visited for the purpose of drawing the tusks. The greatest number that I personally saw round a carcase was five, but when I camped a few hundred yards to windward of some dead elephants we all had a very lively time indeed. Some boys had meat hung up and drying round huge fires too close, as it turned out, to the dead animals. I am safe in saying that from one hour after sundown until one hour before dawn nothing could approach the carcases because of the lions about them. Hyenas and jackals were constantly trying to sneak up to them, only to be chased off with the most terrific growls and rushes by the lions. So impertinent did they become that eventually they occupied with impunity one of the carcases which lay only 15 yds. from the nearest fire. Here they were clearly visible to the boys in the meat camp, and when they first came the boys had tried to drive them off by throwing burning sticks at them. This offensive was so effectually countered by the lions as to cause it to cease at once. The arrival of the first firebrand was greeted with such an appalling outburst of growls, snarls, and showing of teeth as veritably to scare the throwers almost to the point of flight. The lions were not again molested and pursued their scavenging in peace. I spent some days at this spot, as it held the only water for miles around, and one could hear the lions approaching each evening. They commenced to roar about an hour before sundown and continued until they arrived. Where they all disappeared to in the daytime was a mystery, though dogs would have shown them.

This particular camp was also remarkable for the extraordinary number of marabou storks. I had often before seen hundreds of these huge birds collect on a carcase, and I had seen large numbers assembled for the fish which were left high and dry by a receding river, but here they were literally in tens of thousands. And what digestions they have! Huge lumps of elephant offal are snapped up and swallowed. Then when the interior mechanism has received all that it can handle, the foul provender is passed into the great flesh-red sack which depends from the neck. This sack bulges and lengthens until it nearly touches the ground. But what a weary air they have as they flap slowly and heavily away, completely gorged, to a convenient perch, there to digest the putrid mass. As scavengers I should say that five or six marabou would about equal a full-blown incinerator.

As we were so short-handed we found it impossible to cut out the tusks of the elephant we got. Consequently we were obliged to leave them until the action of putrification loosened them in the socket, when they could be drawn. We found that four days were required before this could be done. On the third day the topmost tusk would generally come away, but the under one remained fast. It was owing to this fact that some of our little party had to visit the carcases when they were in a highly advanced state of putrification, and they were invariably found in the possession of one or more lions. Why the lions were such dirty feeders was not apparent. The whole country was seething with game; kob and haartebeeste, giraffe, buffalo, topi and smaller antelope were all numerous. Nearly all cover, such as grass, was burnt off, and it is possible that this made it more difficult for lions to kill.

The skins of these lions were of a peculiarly dark olive tinge for the most part, with the scanty mane of a slightly lighter tint. Some of them were of immense size, and all that we shot were in good condition.

One day our Kabba boy divulged the fact that he had been up the river before. He had come at high water with some companions to gather the leaves of the Borassus palm for making mats. He said that the highest point they had reached lay about a day's travel ahead of us, and then we should reach a country of palms.

We did so. The whole country became covered with these beautiful palms. The huge fruit hung in dozens from the crowns, while the vultures were nesting among the leaves. As our food consisted chiefly of meat and grain, anything in the shape of fruit was eagerly eaten. We used to stew these palm fruits, each the size of a grape fruit. Although the flesh was almost too stringy to swallow, the juice mixed with honey was excellent.

As we plunged along upstream one day, what did we see in mid-stream ahead of us but a floating hippo spear, travelling slowly along with the current towards us. These spears are so constructed that the buoyancy of the shank is sufficient to float about one-third of the spear standing straight up out of the water. This enables the hunter to recover his spear when he misses a hippo.

From this floating evidence it was clear that there were natives in the vicinity, and as we were about to pick up the spear we saw its owner's head watching us from the bank. We salvaged his spear and rested easy, while we tried to talk across the river to him. We tried him in all the native languages known to any member of the safari, but it was not until we tried the Sango tongue of Ubangui watershed that he answered. But he was shy and frightened, and we made little headway. When we offered to bring him his spear he quietly disappeared from view. However, we hoped we had sown good seed by telling him that we were come to hunt elephant, and that all who helped were welcome to the meat. On we went on our way, our progress, as usual, impeded at every pool by hippo. That night we camped on the bank opposite to that of the natives.

Nothing happened. In the morning as we drew out a young water buck was shot for food for the boys—we whites preferred teal. While on the subject of teal I would like to say that we never tired of these birds. We ate them stewed at regular meal times, and we ate them roasted on the spit between meals, cold. We ate them not as we do here, a mere slice or two from the breast ; but we each ate one or two whole birds at a sitting.

As the buck was being skinned we heard a shout from the opposite bank, and there were some natives. This was splendid. On these occasions it is best to show no haste or eagerness, so the skinning and loading of the buck went on methodically. Everything of the buck was taken, as we did not want our newly-found natives to get any meat until we had come to some understanding as to their showing us elephant.

When all were aboard we paddled slowly across to the natives, who were obviously shy. Anchoring the canoe by clinging to the grass, we held a kind of introduction ceremony. Among the natives we were glad to see our friend of yesterday's hippo-spear incident. We laid bare to them our object in ascending this river, and asked in return with whom we had to deal. They said that they came from the south, to reach their village requiring four days' travelling without loads. Knowing the kind of thing they meant by this, I estimated the distance at about 180 or 200 miles. They disclosed also that they had originally been under Senussi at Ndélé, that they still paid taxes and found labour for that post, but that since the occupation of the country by the French, following upon the killing of the old Sultan Senussi, they now lived three or four days' march to the north of the post Ndélé. While Senussi reigned they had been obliged to live in the capital; as with Buba Gida, all the inhabitants of the country for 300 miles round had been "gathered in." Meanwhile, they said, elephant were now in the neighbourhood and that they could show us them. We were ready in a very few moments to accompany them, merely taking a mosquito net, a small packet of tea and sugar and a kettle. Presently we joined up with some more natives, some of whom were armed with the enormous elephant spear of the Arab elephant hunters, whose country lay to the north. These spears have a leaf-shaped head from 7 ins. to 9 ins. across, and are kept razor-edged. The system of hunting is this. In the dry season, when most of the grass has been burnt off and the harmatan is blowing, all the young bloods arrange an expedition. The harmatan is the north-east monsoon of the Indian Ocean, and is a hard breeze at midday of a velocity of about 30 m.p.h., dry and hot when it comes off the desert, and constant as regards direction. At this season so dry is the air that sound carries no distance, and one may walk up to within a few feet of elephant without fear of discovery. These expeditions sometimes number

300 spears. All the old crocks of horses are raked up. The rich are represented on the expedition by slaves, mostly on foot. All are armed with the huge spears, with their bamboo shanks 10 ft. or 12 ft. long. Off they set for the south, poorly supplied with food, as they reckon to live " tough " on what they can kill. When they set out they and the horses are in very good condition, but when they return the men are haggard and thin, leg-weary and footsore, while most of the horses are bleached and well gnawed skeletons in the bush. Few survive the hard work, poor food, and constant attacks of the tsetse fly. When they meet with the fairly recent trail of a herd of elephant they take it up with tremendous vigour, push along it without a stop until dark, camp, on again next day without a stop, perhaps camp again and eventually sight their quarry. Then those on horses dismount, the protectors are taken off the razor-sharp spear-heads, and all advance shoulder to shoulder, spears held projecting 6 ft. or 7 ft. in front, the flat of the spear-head lying in a horizontal direction. With the harmatan blowing its hardest it is possible for the line of spear-men to come within thrusting distance of the elephants' sterns, and at a signal the spears are driven in with the aim of cutting the large tendons and arteries. Hence the width of spear-head. In the consequent commotion casualties among the spear-men are frequent, as might be expected. Off go the unwounded animals, the horses are brought, and the chase is again taken up. Now the elephant will not stop for miles and miles, so they must be ridden to a standstill, or nearly so, before another assault on them can be attempted. Away into desperately dry and waterless country they go, but, try as they may, those human devils are always with them. The hardships these latter bear are almost incredible. They seldom have water or food with them. Often they are starving, and their only hope, the death of an elephant. Kill, or die miserably in the bush, is not a bad system and, as might be expected, leads to perfectly awful destruction of elephant life. Ivory is primarily the object, but, as the hunt develops, water and meat become of more importance. Water, I must explain, is obtained from the elephants'

intestines and, although warm, is quite good to drink. In the average herd cows and calves predominate, consequently they suffer most. In the case of this country the coming of the white man is the indirect cause of the destruction of elephant, and not, as in other parts of Africa, the direct cause of their protection. Natives are permitted to hunt elephant in the above manner on payment of a small fee, in order that they may acquire the wherewithal to pay their taxes—a policy short-sighted indeed, when we remember Darwin's calculation that in 900 years two elephants become a million.

With our newly-found friends as guides we were soon on the trail of our game, and by their aid we ran into and killed late in the afternoon. Our friends were simply overjoyed at the sight of so much meat. They became extremely friendly, cutting grass for my bed, fetching wood and water, ready to do anything. From being rather surly and reserved they became very communicative. As they roasted tit-bits from the elephants on their fires nothing but shouts of laughter and merry chatter could be heard. And when, later, we had all eaten and everyone was smoking—for they carried tobacco— they told me more of themselves. I found that they all talked Sango. They said that every dry season they came to the Bahr Aouck to hunt hippo or elephant, but that so far they had had no luck. During the rains the whole country for miles on either side was under water. No villages existed nearer the river than theirs. They knew the river up to the point where it issued from Lake Mamun. This item was a complete surprise to me, for I had never heard it even suggested that the Bahr Aouck issued from that lake. I pressed my enquiries among the older men, and arrived at the information that shortly after leaving the lake the Bahr Aouck was joined by another river which came from a country I knew to be within the Egyptian Sudan border. I asked after the natives of Lake Mamun, who were supposed to live on the waters themselves, constructing for that purpose huts on piles. They told me that since the slave-raids had ceased, when Senussi was shot by the French, the natives had abandoned their lake dwellings and now lived on the

shores like normal people.   They said that the whole country ahead
was teeming with game.   I had learnt more in half an hour round
the camp-fire with full bellies than weeks of intercourse in the
ordinary way would have yielded.   Such is the power of meat on
the African.

This system of penetrating the country by feeding the natives
has the disadvantage that if you kill a large animal they dry the meat
they cannot eat and take it home to their villages, when it can be
bartered for all kinds of commodities.   Therefore you have constantly
to be making new acquaintances.   Everything else is entirely in its
favour, not the least being its economy.   They will carry light loads
for you for days through the bush, hunt diligently for game, chop out
and carry to the base any ivory you may get.   If you are within fifty
miles or so of villages the women bring food of all sorts, and it is

ARAB SPEAR FOR HAM-STRINGING ELEPHANT.

seldom that a few eggs—more or less fresh—are not forthcoming for
the white man.   Then they hold dances in the camps.   When there
are plenty of young girls about these dances become rather loose
affairs.   The usual restraints of village life seem to be relaxed in
the bush, and everyone enjoys himself or herself to the utmost.
Abundance of animal food has a curious effect on natives.   Where
they inhabit stockless country they go months without flesh, with the
exception of an occasional rat or mongoose or bird.   The craving
for meat becomes intense, and is, in my opinion, the cause of
cannibalism.   Then when they suddenly become possessed of almost
unlimited meat they simply gorge themselves.   A man will eat
15 lb. or 20 lb. in the twenty-four hours.   All night long he eats
and dozes, then eats again.   This turns him a peculiar dull matt
colour and yellow in the eyes.   On the third day he has completely
recovered from this and is again full of energy.   In a very short
time he wants his grain food again, and if he has the choice will eat

a large portion of grain to a small portion of meat. If, as with elephant, there is a good proportion of fat, natives become extremely fit on these rations. As an example of this I can cite the case of a "kilangozi," or head porter, of mine. This man, of slight build, carried a tusk weighing 148 lb. plus his mat, blanket and rations, another 15 lb., for sixty-three days' consecutive marching. The shortest day was five hours, and some were very long indeed. He had as rations throughout this march 2 lb. of native grain each day and as much meat as he cared for with elephant fat. His condition was magnificent throughout.

In the morning I pushed off to look for elephant. The natives promised to cut out the tusks and to bring them to the canoes, which they faithfully did.

After hunting in this region for some days, during which we saw many lion and killed six, we pushed on upstream again. We were soon held up by more elephant and more natives. The news of our doings had already reached the villages south of us, and we had a continuous stream of natives coming hungry to us, carrying our bush loads all over the country, to be rewarded eventually with meat, and then stopping to smoke it while their places were taken by new-comers. So prolific in game was the country that we never reached Lake Mamun, as we had intended. Our time was up, food exhausted and canoes laden. So one fine day we decided to return.

XIII

BUFFALO

THERE is no animal in Africa with such a sinister reputation as the buffalo, whether the bush cow of West Africa or the great black Cape buffalo be under discussion. It has been repeatedly accused of dreadful cunning and great ferocity, and it has undoubtedly caused many deaths and maulings among both white and native hunters. Among the cases which have come under my own observation or of which I have heard from reliable sources, the maulings have been far more numerous than the deaths. The wounds caused by buffalo horns seem to heal better than lion bites; the latter, when made by old lions with dirty teeth, can be very troublesome.

Why the buffalo should have got such an evil name has always rather puzzled me. I have shot hundreds of both kinds during my hunting career, and I have never been charged. And yet I have constantly read of fierce encounters between hunters and their game. Two white men were killed recently in Nigeria by a bush cow, and I have frequently asked for certain natives by name on revisiting villages and have been told that they have been killed by buffalo. Yet, even when I came suddenly on a buffalo bull lying wounded in thick stuff, he did not charge. This animal had been mauled by lion, and according to all the rules should have charged as soon as he became aware of my approach. What he would have done had I not put a bullet through his neck I do not know. Perhaps he might have charged.

I well remember the mixed awe and apprehension with which I approached a herd of buffalo in my early hunting efforts. I had read of all the hair-breadth escapes hunters usually had with these animals, of their diabolical cunning, etc., and I was quite determined not to wound any. I was also very cautious not to approach too near. There were many of them out in fairly short grass. I could see them all clearly, and as we wanted meat I thought I would select a nice fat cow. With me were about forty young bloods from the tribe with which I was hunting. They were all fully armed in their fashion—each man carried two thrusting spears and a rhino or giraffe hide shield. The reason they carried shields was that we had been hunting elephant in no man's land, where prowlers from the enemy, *i.e.*, the neighbouring tribe, might have been met. Telling this mob to get away back while I did the shooting I left them and approached the browsing and unsuspicious herd. Selecting what I thought would be a fat one, I fired. Without pausing or wavering the whole herd started straight for me, closing together as they came. I fired again at one of the leaders and then started to get out of their way. As I ran to the side I met and ran through the forty spearmen, who were now rushing straight to meet the herd. Stopping and turning, I was astounded to see these fellows right in among the buffalo, some retreating cleverly backwards and receiving the charging animals' rushes on their shields, while others jabbed spears into their vitals from the sides. No sooner was an animal down than off they went after the retreating herd. And here, again, all my preconceived notions were upset, for the natives caught up with the buffalo again and killed several more. But for the herd's arrival at a belt of forest, perhaps they would all have been speared. Not a native was touched. I must say I was rather staggered by what had taken place; the awe-inspiring charge was apparently a simple running away; the terrific speed, strength and agility of the story-book buffalo all shown up by a handful of nimble lads armed with soft iron spears; the formidable buffalo made to cut a very poor figure, and the white man with his wonderful gun made to look extremely foolish.

This incident put me right about buffalo, I think, for I have killed scores and scores since, and I have never had any trouble with them. I have shot them in West Africa, where they are usually met in thick stuff and in long grass, and also in the Liberian forests, east of the Nile and in the Congo—and invariably with small bores. The most killing bullet I found to be the solid.

The stampede or rush straight towards the shot was a fairly frequent occurrence in my experience ; and if one were convinced that the animals were charging, one would have to write down the buffalo as an extremely dangerous animal were it not for the ease with which they are killed with end-on delivered solid bullets. Of course, flesh wounds are no good. The vitals *must be raked*. But in thick stuff the target is so close and so big that no one should miss it, as for all game of this nature a reliable magazine rifle is streets ahead of a double. In a mix-up with buffalo in bush it is sometimes necessary to fire four or even five shots in rapid succession, and for this the double is mere handicap.

Much has been written about the difference in colour among buffalo, and there have been attempts to separate them into different races. How all the colours may be found in one herd may be witnessed on the Shari River in the dry season when the grass has been burned. I have shot a grey bull, a black bull, a red and a fawn-coloured bull from the same herd, all fully adult. And I shot them after watching the herd through glasses for fully half an hour, during which time I saw many of each of the above colours. It must not be supposed that this was an isolated instance of these colours happening in the same herd, for every time I saw any considerable number of big buffalo in open country I have observed the same sprinkling of colours.

The jet black is the colour of the solitary bulls one meets casually, and I imagine from that that black is the final colour.

As with the semi-wild domesticated cattle of the ranching districts of America, the sight or smell of blood seems to infuriate buffalo more than anything. On one occasion when in want of meat I hit a cow buffalo in the lungs with a ·22 high-velocity bullet. She was one of a small herd, and as she staggered about in her death agony all the others, including the calves and yearlings, went for her, goring her and knocking her about and completely hiding her from me. They were dreadfully excited, bellowing and roaring and even butting at one another.

Natives of almost all tribes have far less respect for buffalo than the white hunters. They will attack buffalo with very primitive weapons. I remember once going after an old bull buffalo which had spent the night in a native garden. Two middle-aged natives tracked for me. Each carried an abnormal number of short spears, for what purpose I did not understand until later. They tracked well and quickly as the dew was still on the ground, and wherever the buffalo had passed was a perfectly plain track. We presently came to a large depression filled with high reeds well over a man's head. Here, the natives said, we were sure to find our game. Now, at this time I was still in my novitiate as regards buffalo, and my head was stuffed with the nonsense one is usually told about these animals. Consequently, I was rather surprised that the natives should be still willing to go out into the reed-bed. However, I thought it was up to me to lead the way, and I did so for a few yards, when we got into such a maze of buffalo tracks and runs and tunnels that I was obliged to let one of the natives re-find the tracks and lead the way. This he did quite cheerfully, handing to his companion his surplus spears. On we went into the most appalling stuff—reeds fourteen feet or fifteen feet high, and so strong and dense that one could not force one's way along except in the buffalo runs. Visibility was good for about two yards ahead. I felt very uncomfortable indeed, but what gave me confidence was that the leading native was quite at ease, and I kept thinking that he ought to know all about buffalo, if anyone did. Personally I expected to see infuriated buffalo suddenly appearing at a yard's range at any moment.

We went very quietly, and after prowling for half an hour the leader stopped. We stood listening, and there, as it were almost at arm's length, was a heavy breathing. The tracker leant gently to one side to let me pass, and I crept cautiously forward. I must confess that I was in a mortal funk. I felt sure that a frightful charge was imminent. The breathing could not be more than eight yards or ten yards distant, and yet nothing was visible. When I had covered, I suppose, five yards or so there was a terrific snort and a rushing kind of crash. I had my rifle up covering the noise, ready in an instant to loose off. Nothing appeared because the buffalo was in as great a state of terror as I was, and was off. This fact gave me great confidence, as did also the eagerness with which my companions took up the trail. We tracked and tracked that wretched buffalo until he must have been in a frightful state of nerves. We came to within hearing distance of him frequently, but never saw him. My confidence grew by leaps and bounds, and I tried rushing at him as soon as we knew he was close. This almost succeeded as I saw the reeds still in motion where they had closed after his passage.

On the way home I stopped with a spear point almost touching my shirt front. The cheery fellows with me had planted their spears in the buffalo runs pointing in the direction from which they thought the buffalo might come—and extraordinarily difficult they were to see, presented, as they were, point on.

My experience of buffalo is that they are worthy game in thick stuff, but ludicrously easy things to kill in open country. Any form of expanding bullet should not be used, although for a broadside shot any kind of bullet is good enough. But if one carries mixed bullets one is certain sooner or later to find oneself loaded with just the wrong type of bullet, and, perhaps, with no time to change. I have always found the solid very deadly for all kinds of game. An end-on shot suits this type of bullet to perfection, as the vitals are certain to be raked if the holding is as it should be. Blind terror-stricken rushes by buffalo are not uncommonly straight towards the gun, but the brutes are easily dropped with a well planted shot. I believe that buffalo can be very nasty when in thick stuff with a flesh wound, but there is no earthly reason with modern firearms why one should miss such a target as is presented by a buffalo's vitals. Always know where you are sending your bullet, I have found to be an excellent maxim.

XIV

AFRICAN LIONS

AFRICAN lions may be placed in two categories—those which kill their game, and those which live largely on carrion, as hyenas do. Among the former, carrion-eaters will sometimes be found, but this foul feeding is generally due to old age or broken teeth, and it is among these that the habit of man-eating takes place. While in robust health and full possession of their power these lions will never touch dead meat, preferring to kill zebra, haartebeeste, wildebeeste, or even buffalo or giraffe; whereas the pig-eaters—as the lions of the second category are called—prey upon much smaller stuff, such as warthog, reedbuck, duiker, etc., failing which they will eat anything dead they may find. There are, therefore, lions and pig-eating lions.

Lions are much finer, bolder and more courageous than the pig-eaters. At night they will attack cattle inside strong zerebas in spite of fires, shouts and shots. When they take to man-eating they do it thoroughly, as, for instance, the two or three old lions which terrorised the coolie camps at Tsavo during the construction of the Uganda Railway. These accounted for some scores of victims in spite of colossal thorn zerebas, fires and armed guards. Their doings are recounted in the " Man Eaters of Tsavo," and I will only add to that able account the doings of an old Sikh ex-soldier and his son. It was when the Government had offered a large reward for every lion killed within a mile on either side of the railway. Fired with the prospect of immediate wealth, this old man obtained a Rigby-Mauser ·275, and he and his son took to hunting lions. There were then in East Africa troops of lions sometimes over twenty strong. Knowing from the permanent-way gangs of coolies the likeliest spots, the hunters began their operations. These consisted of building shelters from which to fire by night, and they were generally situated close to reed beds known to be used by lions. At first the shelters were quite elaborate affairs affording considerable protection. Familiarity taught them that no protection was necessary, and latterly the cache was merely a ring of boulders over which one could fire from the prone position. The old man could imitate a goat or a cow to perfection, but whether it was desire on the part of the lions to eat goat or cow, or merely curiosity to find out what the strange noise was, must remain a mystery. Certain it is, though, that the Sikhs' cache was a sure draw. The young fellow shot straight and true, and lion after lion succumbed. In nine months these two men claimed the reward on some ninety skins. On about forty-five the reward was actually paid, there being some doubt as to whether the remainder were killed within the mile limit.

As East Africa became better known, sportsmen came in greater numbers for big game, and many lions were killed. At this period some extraordinary bags were made. The hunting was done entirely on foot, and it was not until later that the use of ponies and dogs for hunting lions became common. Sometimes the natives could be induced to drive them out of their strongholds, the great reed beds of the Stony Athy. To do this armed only with spears requires some nerve, as most men who have entered these reed beds will admit, even when armed with modern rifles. The reeds are not the little short things we know in this country, but great high strong grass well over a man's head.

This hunting of lions by men who were novices at the game was attended by many casualties. I was told that in one year out of about forty visiting sportsmen who devoted themselves seriously to lion hunting, twenty were mauled. Of these twenty, more than half were killed or died from the effects of wounds. The lions of that period were extraordinarily bold and courageous. In the early morning on those huge plains I have walked steadily towards a troop of lions numbering a score. Just as steadily walked away the troop—no hurry or fear of man. When I ran, a magnificent male deliberately turned and stood facing me. As I approached he advanced quietly towards me, while the others idled along in the opposite direction. One could hardly imagine a finer sight than this great bold fellow facing the rising sun on the dead open plain. But it was futile swagger on his part, for he was not a man-eater. He had killed and eaten to repletion like all the lions on those plains. And yet, there he was, deliberately advancing without cause or reason. This is the only instance in my experience of a lion, as it were, meeting one; more often they are off to cover, although when pursued and pressed they will sometimes turn.

The reason of the high mortality among those who hunt lions casually is, I think, the simple one of not holding straight enough. Buck-fever or excitement, coupled with anxiety lest the animal should slip away, is probably the cause of much of the erratic shooting done at lions. This frequently results in flesh wounds or stomach wounds, which very often cause the lion to make a determined charge; and there are a great many things easier to hit than a charging lion. Great care should be taken to plant the bullet right. The calibre does not matter, I am convinced, provided the bullet is in the right place. Speaking personally, I have killed sixteen lions with ·256 and ·275 solid bullets, and, as far as I can recollect, none of them required a second shot. One showed no sign of having been hit. This was a lioness which galloped across my front. I was carrying a Mannlicher-Schonauer ·256 loaded with solids. I let drive at her and she carried on as if untouched. I thought that I had missed her clean, until I found her some way further on, stone dead. Search as I would, nowhere could I find either entrance or exit bullet hole, and it was not until she was skinned that I found the tiny wound channel through the kidneys. This lioness had had a companion lioness, and in the evening as I was pottering about I was astonished to see her walking round the flayed carcase of her dead friend: both of them were very old. When lions have cubs and are disturbed they will sometimes show fight. I have seen a native severely chased in one direction while the cubs scuttled away in the other. I do not think that the lioness really meant business, as it would have been an easy matter for her to have caught the native. She merely scared the wits out of the lad by bounding leisurely along, growling and snarling in an alarming manner.

Lions in their encounters with game frequently come by nasty wounds, as almost any old lion skin will show. They are often bested by buffalo, and this is not surprising when one considers the weight and strength of an adult Cape buffalo. The surprising thing is that an animal weighing 300 lb. to 400 lb. should ever be capable of overcoming such a powerful, active and heavy one as the buffalo. But, probably—as Selous observed—lions attack buffaloes *en masse* and not singly.

The oryx, with their scimitar-like horns, occasionally kill lions outright. These beautiful antelope are extraordinarily dexterous in getting their 3-ft. horns down from the normal position, where they almost sweep their backs, until the points are presented almost straight in front. This movement is so quick as to be scarcely visible. Lions have been found pierced from side to side.

In country where game is very plentiful lions are distinctly casual in their hunting. I have seen one rush at a zebra, stop when within about ten paces of it, and turn indifferently away. When I first saw him he was about thirty or forty paces from the zebra, and he covered the twenty or so yards at terrific speed.

As a game animal the lion affords first-class sport, and sportsmen will be glad that some protection has been given lions in East Africa. This, combined with the large stock in the game reserves, should ensure good sport for many years to come.

XV

RIFLES

THE question of which rifles to use for big-game hunting is for each individual to settle for himself. If the novice starts off with, say, three rifles: one heavy, say a double ·577; one medium, say a ·318 or a ·350; and one light, say a ·256 or a ·240 or a ·276, then he cannot fail to develop a preference for one or other of them.

For the style of killing which appeals to me most the light calibres are undoubtedly superior to the heavy. In this style you keep perfectly cool and are never in a hurry. You never fire unless you can clearly see your way to place the bullet in a vital spot. That done the calibre of the bullet makes no difference. But to some men of different temperament this style is not suited. They cannot or will not control the desire to shoot almost on sight if close to the game. For these the largest bores are none too big. If I belonged to this school I would have had built a much more powerful weapon than the ·600 bores.

Speaking personally, my greatest successes have been obtained with the 7 mm. Rigby-Mauser or ·276, with the old round-nosed solid, weighing, I believe, 200 grs. It seemed to show a remarkable aptitude for finding the brain of an elephant. This holding of a true course I think is due to the moderate velocity, 2,300 ft., and to the fact that the proportion of diameter to length of bullet seems to be the ideal combination. For when you come below ·276 to ·256 or 6·5 mm., I found a bending of the bullet took place when fired into heavy bones.

Then, again, the ballistics of the ·275 cartridge, as loaded in Germany at any rate, are such as to make for the very greatest reliability. In spite of the pressures being high, the cartridge construction is so excellent that trouble from blowbacks and split cases and loose caps in the mechanism are entirely obviated. Why the caps should be so reliable in this particular cartridge I have never understood. But the fact remains that, although I have used almost every kind of rifle, the only one which never let me down was a ·276 with German (D.W.M.) ammunition. I never had one single hang-fire even. Nor a stuck case, nor a split one, nor a blowback, nor a miss-fire. All of these I had with other rifles.

I often had the opportunity of testing this extraordinary little weapon on other animals than elephant. Once, to relate one of the less bloody of its killings, I met at close range, in high grass, three bull buffalo. Having at the moment a large native following more or less on the verge of starvation, as the country was rather gameless, I had no hesitation about getting all three. One stood with head up about 10 yds. away and facing me, while the others appeared as rustles in the grass behind him. Instantly ready as I always was, carrying my own rifle, I placed a ·276 solid in his chest. He fell away in a forward lurch, disclosing another immediately behind him and in a similar posture. He also received a ·276, falling on his nose and knees. The third now became visible through the commotion, affording a chance at his neck as he barged across my front. A bullet between neck and shoulder laid him flat. All three died without further trouble, and the whole affair lasted perhaps four or five seconds.

Another point in favour of the ·276 is the *shortness* of the motions required to reload. This is most important in thick stuff. If one develops the habit by constant practice of pushing the rifle forward with the left hand while the right hand pulls back the bolt and then *vice versa* draws the rifle towards one while closing it, the rapidity of fire becomes quite extraordinary. With a long cartridge, necessitating long bolt movements, there is a danger that on occasions requiring great speed the bolt may not be drawn back quite sufficiently far to reject the fired case, and it may become re-entered into the chamber. This once happened to me with a ·350 Mauser at very close quarters with a rhino. I did not want any rhino, but the villagers had complained about this particular one upsetting their women while gathering firewood. We tracked him back into high grass. I had foolishly allowed a number of the villagers to come with me. When it was obvious that we were close to our game these villagers began their African whispering, about as loud, in the still bush, as a full-throated bass voice in a gramophone song. Almost immediately the vicious old beast could be heard tearing through the grass straight towards us. I meant to fire my first shot into the movement as soon as it became visible, and to kill with my second as he swerved. At a very few paces' distance the grass showed where he was and I fired into it, reloading almost instantaneously. At the shot he swerved across, almost within kicking range, showing a wonderful chance at his neck. I fired, but there was only a click. I opened the bolt and there was my empty case.

I once lost a magnificent bull elephant through a ·256 Mannlicher going wrong. I got up to him and pulled trigger on him, but click ! a miss-fire. He paid no attention and I softly opened the bolt. Out came the case, spilling the flake powder into the mechanism and leaving the bullet securely fast in the barrel lead. I tried to ram another cartridge in, but could not do so. Here was a fix. How to get that bullet out. Calibre ·256 is very small when you come to try poking sticks down it. Finally I got the bullet out, but then the barrel was full of short lengths of sticks which could not be cleared out, as no stick could be found sufficiently long, yet small enough. So I decided to chance it and fire the whole lot into the old elephant, who, meanwhile, was feeding steadily along. I did so from suffi-ciently close range, but what happened I cannot say. Certainly that elephant got nothing of the charge except perhaps a few bits of stick. That something had touched him up was evident from his anxiety to get far away, for he never stopped during the hours I followed him.

At one time I used a double ·450-·400. It was a beautiful

weapon, but heavy. Its drawbacks I found were : it was slow for
the third and succeeding shots ; it was noisy ; the cartridges weighed
too much ; the strikers broke if a shade too hard or flattened and cut.
the cap if a shade too soft ; the caps of the cartridges were quite
unreliable ; and finally, if any sand, grit or vegetation happened to
fall on to the breech faces as you tore along you were done ; you could
not close it. Grit especially was liable to do this when following an
elephant which had had a mud bath, leaving the vegetation covered
with it as he passed along. This would soon dry and tumble off at
the least touch.

I have never heard any explanation of the undoubted fact that
our British ammunition manufacturers cannot even yet produce a
reliable rifle cartridge head, anvil and cap, other than that of the
service ·303. On my last shoot in Africa two years ago, when W.
and I went up the Bahr Aouck, the very first time he fired at an
elephant he had a miss-fire and I had identically the same thing.
We were using ·318's with English made cartridges. Then on the
same shoot I nearly had my head blown off and my thumb severely
bruised by an English loaded ·256. There was no miss-fire there.
The cartridge appeared to me almost to detonate. More vapour
came from the breech end than from the other. I have since been
told by a great authority that it was probably due to a burst case, due
to weak head. On my return I complained about this and was
supplied with a new batch, said to be all right. But whenever I fire
four or five rounds I have a jamb, and on investigating invariably
find a cap blown out and lodging in the slots cut for the lugs of the
bolt head. Luckily these cartridges are wanting in force ; at one
time they used fairly to blast me with gas from the wrong end. The
fact that these faults are not conspicuously apparent in this country
may be traced to the small number of rounds fired from sporting
rifles, or, more probably, to the pressures increasing in a tropical
temperature.

I have never been able to appreciate " shock " as applied to
killing big game. It seems to me that you cannot hope to kill an

elephant weighing six tons by "shock" unless you hit him with a field gun. And yet nearly all writers advocate the use of large bores as they "shock" the animal so much more than the small bores. They undoubtedly "shock" the firer more, but I fail to see the difference they are going to make to the recipient of the bullet. If you expect to produce upon him by the use of big bores the effect a handful of shot had upon the Jumping Frog of Calaveras County, you will be disappointed. Wounded non-vitally he will go just as far and be just as savage with 500 grains of lead as with 200. And 100 grains in the right place are as good as ten million.

The thing that did most for my rifle shooting was, I believe, the fact that I always carried my own rifle. It weighed about 7 lb., and I constantly aligned it at anything and everything. I was always playing with it. Constant handling, constant aiming, constant Swedish drill with it, and then when it was required there it was ready and pointing true.

XVI

AFRICAN ADMINISTRATIONS

MY object in writing this is to contrast the different administrations I have come in touch with during my hunting. I have made no deep study of the matter and simply record the impressions I received. The French system of administering native races in Africa appears to differ fundamentally from the British. They look upon country they occupy as conquered territory, and anyone may buy it or lease it who wishes; whereas, in West Africa at any rate, the British consider the country as belonging to the natives, and it is extremely difficult for a white man to acquire land.

When the French take over a new country they occupy it most efficiently. We frequently are contented to paint it red on the map, close it up to trade and leave it simmering, as it were, in its own juice of savagery. This appears to lead to considerable trouble ultimately, for firearms are liable to find their way in, or the country gets raided white. When the French have to deal with a new country a special force of military character—Colonial Army it is called—takes it over by marching into it and establishing posts. If this force encounters obstruction, so much the sooner will the country be subjugated. Terrorise or kill the present generation and educate the next generation, and in course of time you have a race of black Frenchmen. In the fullness of time perfect equality is given her black citizens, as anyone may see at Dakar in West Africa.

Here we have a modern town which might be anywhere in France. Remarkable docks and landing arrangements strike one first. Then the houses and *cafés*. French whites and French blacks apparently on perfect equality. I was told that Dakar elected a black Deputy to send to France. Every black speaks French—real French, not like our pidgin English. And their blacks are so polite; perfect manners. Contrast this with the following; it happened to me at Sierra Leone, one of our most " advanced " black possessions :

I was travelling by tramp steamer—the only passenger. As we dropped anchor I was leaning on the rail looking at the town and shipping, when, directly below me, I saw a black stoker crawl slowly out of the coaling port and coolly dive into the sea, when he struck out for the land. I thought he was a stowaway and wished him luck and thought nothing more about it. Some time after, the captain asked me if I had seen a boy jump overboard, and I admitted I had. He then told me that that boy had been to the magistrate, had sworn that he had been thrown overboard and much more to the effect that he had been half murdered, etc. The magistrate had summoned the captain and the chief engineer, and they asked me to go as a witness. We went ashore at the appointed time, and never have I seen natives so badly out of hand. At the landing place we were met by a mob of sympathisers of the boy's, or, in reality, a mob of natives actively hostile to whites and not afraid to show it. In the Court House itself there was more or less peace. At any rate, the howling was confined to the outside of the building. I gave evidence to the effect that I had seen the boy drop quietly into the water apparently of his own volition. The result was given against the ship, whether justly or not I do not pretend to judge. But when we three proceeded to leave the Court our appearance was greeted in such a way by the mob outside as to send the captain back in alarm. Under police escort we went, with perhaps two hundred howling blacks baiting us the whole way. Now this scene would be unthinkable under any other flag. It may be the result of even-handed justice, but, I ask, what good does it do? Those blacks hated us and had no respect for us or any other white man.

Lest from the above remarks on French administrative methods it be thought that I am in favour of them, I would like to say that, on the contrary, I think that all wild tribes suffer by contact with any

Western culture. All their old customs, many of which were good and all binding, go, and in their place we substitute English or Indian law, which is entirely unsuited to the African. But if we must go there, I honestly think that the French method entails least suffering in the long run.

It was my lot to travel in the German Cameroons while still under German rule. There every black was required to remove his hat when *any* white passed. This simple little law was undoubtedly good, at any rate for the first few generations of contact; and the natives appeared to me to be happier and much more contented in the Cameroons than anywhere else I have been. We say that we do not tolerate the brutality which French and German methods entail. And we do not do so directly. But under our system of employing and paying native chiefs and kings to gather taxes and to settle disputes we blind ourselves if we do not recognise that far worse injustices and cruelties go on than could ever happen under direct white administration, however corrupt.

In the Sudan I came in contact with, to me, quite a new idea of governing native races. It happened thus : I and a companion had arrived from Abyssinia by native dug-out. We came down the Gelo into the Pibor and then down the Sobat until that river joined the Nile. Just before its junction there was an American Mission Station. As we were floating leisurely down towards this, the boy steering one of our canoes was seized by a crocodile and pulled off the stern. The other occupant had a gun and let fly in the air. The crocodile abandoned his victim, who swam back and clambered on to the canoe. When we arrived we saw at once that the boy was very badly mauled, and we paddled him down to the Mission Station. There the doctor did what he could for him ; but the poor fellow died soon afterwards. The Mission people told us that if we wished to dispose of our canoes they would gladly buy them, as wooden canoes were almost priceless on the Nile. In return for their kindness we promised to give them our canoes after we had unloaded them at Tewfikia Post.

We proceeded to Tewfikia and found it a large and well-laid-out military post. One of the crack Sudanese regiments, picked officers, grand mess, band; altogether a show place. Sentries on the bank, too. Well, we were most hospitably received, and I hasten to add here that no one there was to blame for the ridiculous thing that now happened. It was the fault of the man or men who had evolved this unique and wonderful system of governing native tribes.

We drew our flotilla of canoes up to the bank at a spot indicated, where there was a sentry who would keep an eye on our gear, which was mostly ivory. We off-loaded this, so that the canoes should be ready for our friends of the Mission. As the band was playing in the evening the natives came and stole all our canoes under the very noses of not only the sentry, but numerous other people. They were certainly lying not more than thirty yards from the mess.

The theft created a tremendous flutter, but no one seemed to know what to do. All was utter chaos. Eventually someone was found who knew of a chief, and he was sent for. He refused to come in. And then I heard that the policy of the Government (sic) was to leave the natives alone. I was told that this was carried out to the extent of allowing pitched battles between tribes to be fought on the large plain opposite the post, and the wounded of both sides were left to be tended in Tewfikia hospital.

We never heard that the canoes were recovered. This is the kind of thing that makes for trouble in the future, in my humble opinion. Far better clear out and let someone else have a try.

INDEX

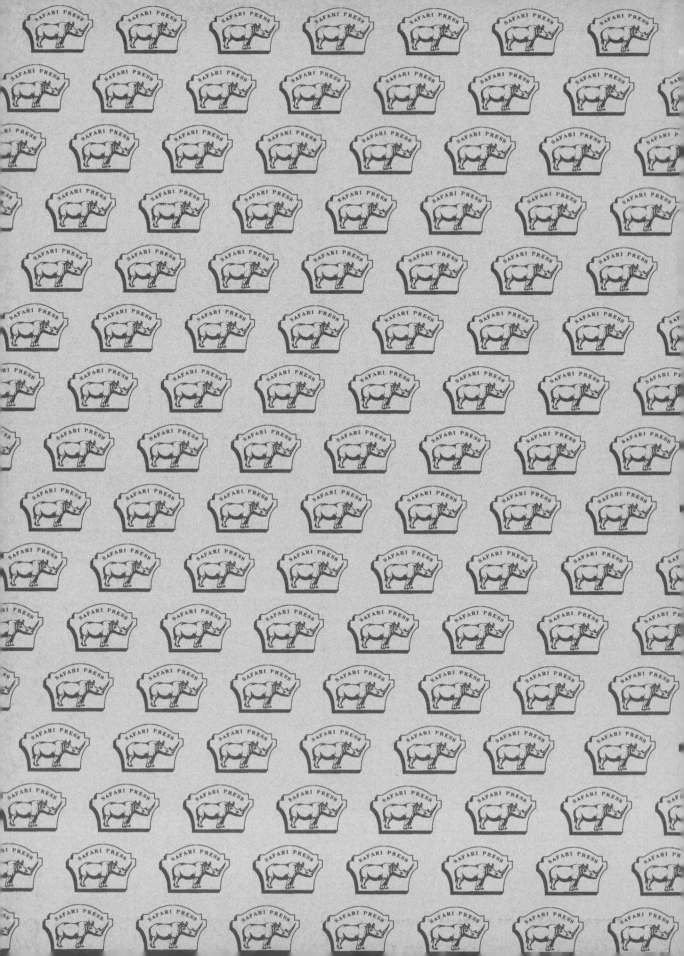